THE
McVITIE'S
BOOK OF BETTER
BAKING

MARY NORWAK

A MARTIN BOOK

**Pictured on front cover
and title page:**
Top left Chocolate Rum Cake (p. 108); *Top right* Game Pie (p. 83); *Bottom left* Milk Twist (p. 42); *Bottom right* Kugelhopf (p. 62)

Published by Martin Books, an imprint of Woodhead-Faulkner Ltd, Fitzwilliam House, 32 Trumpington Street, Cambridge CB2 1QY, in association with UB (Biscuits) Ltd, Syon Lane, Isleworth, Middlesex TW7 5NN

First published 1987
© Woodhead-Faulkner Ltd 1987

Norwak, Mary
 The McVitie's book of better baking.
 1. Baking
 I. Title
 641.7'1   TX765
 ISBN 0-85941-373-X

Design: Carrods Graphic Design
Photography: Laurie Evans and John Lee
Stylist: Lesley Richardson (for Laurie Evans)
Food preparation for photography: Jane Suthering and Ann Page-Wood
Line drawings: Richard Jacobs
Decorative illustrations: Sal Garfi
Typesetting: Rowland Phototypesetting Ltd, Bury St Edmunds
Printed and bound in Singapore

*F*oreword

Baking has been our most useful cooking method for as long as wheat
and other cereals have been the nutritious mainstays of our daily
diet. But the art of baking has gone a very long way since the ancient
times when King Alfred burned the cakes.

Baking is now far more exciting and enjoyable than
ever before. There are more ingredients to choose from and
ovens barely resemble those of the past. Some of the
greatest changes took place in the nineteenth century,
when people took their dinners to be cooked at public
bake-houses, and it was at this time that the great bakeries
were born.

McVitie's have been baking biscuits and cakes since
the 1830s and many of their recipes are the result of years of
perfecting the baking craft.

Today there is enormous scope for baking in the home.
Ovens have never before been so accurate and, when they
are used with the correct cooking techniques, you can
produce perfect results every time. Microwave ovens, for
example, open up completely new possibilities and you can
try the recipes specially designed for microwave cooking
from the chapter on this subject.

Mary Norwak is an expert on traditional cooking and
she has brought together recipes for the best of the world's
breads, cakes, biscuits and other baked dishes for this
remarkable collection. This book not only contains a
wealth of delicious recipes but will also show you,
step-by-step, how to produce perfect finished results.

McVitie's are delighted to be associated with this work
on home baking, which not only acts as a practical cookery
guide but can also be treasured for its fine appreciation of
baking as a master craft.

McVITIE'S

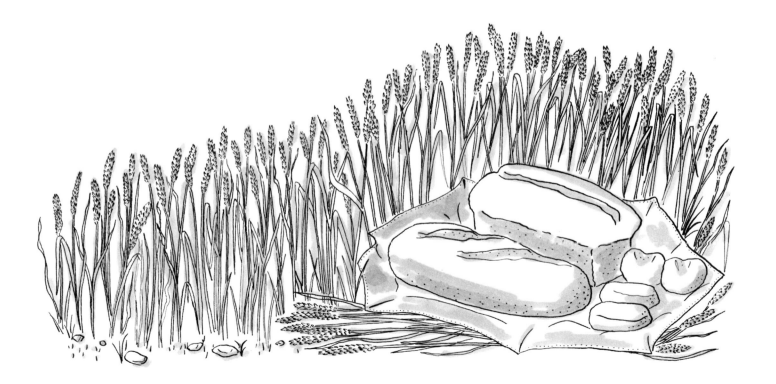

Contents

FOREWORD 3

INTRODUCTION 6

INGREDIENTS, NUTRITION
AND BAKING
EQUIPMENT 7

BASIC METHODS OF
OVEN BAKING 13

BAKING WITHOUT
AN OVEN 19

MICROWAVE BAKING 27

BREADS AND ROLLS 37

TEABREADS
AND BUNS 49

YEAST PASTRY AND
BATTER BAKES 57

PASTRY 65

PIES AND FLANS 77

BISCUITS AND
COOKIES 85

CAKES 95

BAKING FOR SPECIAL
OCCASIONS 111

ICINGS, FILLINGS AND
DECORATION 119

FREEZING REMINDERS 126

INDEX 127

Recipe Notes
Quantities are given in all
recipes for both metric
(g, ml, etc.) and imperial
(oz, pints, etc.) measures.
Use either, but not both, in
any one recipe. All spoon
measures are level and the
eggs used are medium
(size 3) unless otherwise
stated. Preparation and
cooking times are given
as guidelines and are
approximate.

*I*ntroduction

Baking is one of the most satisfying culinary arts, for the results look beautiful and are delicious to eat. The natural baker is a relaxed person who creates from simple ingredients minor masterpieces that please the eye as well as the palate.

While baking is an art, it is also an exact science, because successful results depend on precise measurements, carefully balanced ingredients and an understanding of the action of heat. Although a successful casserole or pudding may consist of the old-fashioned 'bit of this and bit of that', perfect bread, cakes and biscuits can only be achieved by careful attention to detail.

Such care need not be exhausting or off-putting: all you need to do is follow a good recipe exactly, choosing the correct ingredients, and measuring and assembling them as instructed. Problems arise only if the cook is slipshod, and does not use the recommended tin size or oven temperature, for example.

In these diet-conscious days, we are all aware that over-indulgence in some foods can result in overweight. But home-baked cakes, bread, biscuits and pastry are made from pure and nourishing ingredients, and many variations may be made using wholemeal flour, oats, honey, nuts and dried fruit which provide additional nutrients and also dietary fibre, which is vital to a healthy diet, especially for the weight-conscious (see page 10).

Everyone is delighted with the results of baking, whether a gorgeous crusty bread for everyday use, crisp biscuits in the lunch-box, a steak and kidney pie for a weekend meal, or a farmhouse cake for a rare moment of relaxation at Sunday teatime. Home baking gives great pleasure to the cook and to those who eat the results, and it is a creative experience which is thoroughly satisfying and very rewarding.

Many of the recipes in this book are kitchen classics, but I have included both traditional regional dishes and family favourites as well as some unfamiliar and exotic dishes. We are exceptionally lucky in these modern times to have a huge range of cookers and baking equipment and high-quality ingredients, but we are also short of time. Happily, we can take advantage of the microwave oven, the food processor and the blender to speed up processes, and the refrigerator and freezer to store the results of a bake-in for future use. Even the novice cook can tackle the most traditional recipes quickly and efficiently, and the time you spend in the kitchen, as well as the results of your baking, should be enjoyable and satisfying.

Before using the recipes, take a few minutes to read the basic information and baking hints, and then choose a recipe and read it carefully. Gather the ingredients and equipment, spend a happy half-hour creating something delicious, and you'll be eager for another baking session and the chance to perfect further skills. Happy baking!

MARY NORWAK

*I*ngredients,
nutrition and
baking
equipment

*A*ll baking ingredients must be fresh and of high quality, as stale flour, eggs and fat can impart most unpleasant flavours. It is better to buy small quantities of ingredients and to store them carefully than to indulge in bulk-buying and to find that raw materials have deteriorated after some months. Flour should be stored in a jar or tin, surplus fats in the refrigerator or freezer and eggs in a cool place rather than in the refrigerator.

Flour

This essential baking ingredient is available in many varieties, but if space is limited, plain white flour is best for recipes. Self-raising flour is used in some recipes, but plain flour and a raising agent are more traditional and give excellent results. Finely sifted flours are best for sponges. Wholemeal flour may be used for fruit cakes and gingerbreads as a substitute for white flour, but a little more liquid will be necessary to prevent the results being heavy, dry and solid. If a recipe is not specially formulated for wholemeal flour and you would like to try it, substitute wholemeal flour for half the white flour and see how it affects the texture and flavour. After a little experimentation, try using all wholemeal flour and you will have become sufficiently familiar with the recipe to know how much extra liquid is necessary to get the right effect.

For bread-making, the flour must be made from strong, hard wheat, whether it is white or wholemeal, as this develops a stronger cell structure which supports rising bread. This flour is now generally sold as bread flour, but may be labelled 'strong flour'. Some cooks like to use this flour for batters and for puff and choux pastry because it gives volume and a light texture.

Wholemeal flour contains all the wheatgrain and is described as 100% extraction flour. Wheatmeal or brown flour contains 80–90% of the cleaned wheatgrain, with more bran than white flour. Wheatgerm flour has up to 10% extra wheatgerm added. Granary flour contains added bran and wheatgrains (and the name is registered by RHM PLC). Stoneground flour is produced by the traditional method of grinding between two horizontal stones, but most flour is produced by modern roller milling. Bran, which has been extracted during the making of white flour, may be purchased separately and added to recipes to give a greater fibre content.

Other Cereals

Our flour is made from wheat grains, but rye, barley and oats may be used in recipes, as may cornmeal. These special flours are obtainable from many grocers and from health food shops. Rolled oats, breakfast cereals and muesli are also useful for some recipes to give flavour and texture as well as extra fibre.

Raising Agents

Baking powder is quick to use and gives mixtures a light texture. *Bicarbonate of soda* is the usual raising agent when honey, black treacle and sour milk are used, as it helps to neutralise acids and gives a soft cake. It may be combined with *cream of tartar* in cake-bread mixtures such as scones and has the same effect as baking powder.

Yeast was the original raising agent, in the form of a sloppy 'barm' from beer, which imparted a strong flavour to bread and cakes. Today's baker's yeast looks like putty and may be bought at health food shops and some bakers. It should be creamy in colour, cool to the touch and easy to break. It will keep fresh if tied in a polythene bag and stored in a cool place for 5 days (1 month in a refrigerator; 6 months in a freezer). Brewer's yeast, and autolysed and tonic yeasts are not suitable for baking.

Dried yeast is available in cans and packages from health food stores, grocers and chemists. It will keep for up to 6 months in an airtight container in a cool place, but it loses its power quickly if there is air space in a container and will not remain active. A new type of yeast called *easy-blend dried yeast* is available in sealed packets; it is very easy to use, as it is stirred directly into the dry ingredients before any liquid is added. If this type of yeast is used, it is important to follow the manufacturer's instructions on the quantity required and the method to be followed, as it will not work if reconstituted like ordinary dried yeast.

Sugar and Other Sweeteners

A wide variety of sugar and sweetening agents may be used in baking. *Granulated sugar* is used for rubbed-in mixtures and for fruit cakes. *Caster sugar* must be used for sponge cakes because it dissolves quickly in creamed or whisked mixtures. *Icing sugar* is only for icings, except for one or two biscuit mixtures where a velvety texture is required. *Natural brown sugars* which are unrefined may vary from light to dark in colour and from a texture like sand to one like toffee, and they are excellent for fruit cakes and spice cakes. *Demerara sugar* is seldom used for baking because of its gritty texture, but it is useful for decorating the surface of cakes and biscuits. *Golden syrup* is very sweet and is used in a few cakes but does not affect colour or texture. *Black treacle* gives a rich, dark colour and distinctive toffee flavour. *Honey* also has a distinctive flavour, but causes darkening during cooking. If it is to be used instead of sugar in a standard recipe, only one-third of the total should be honey, or the texture and flavour will not be attractive.

Fats

A wide variety of fats is available, and each gives a characteristic flavour to baked goods, as well as altering the texture. *Butter* has a beautiful flavour, but is not very easy to cream, and produces a slightly heavy cake. It is, however, particularly good in biscuits where a delicate flavour is more noticeable than in cakes, and unsalted butter gives particularly delicious results.

Block margarine is excellent for rubbed-in cakes, and may be used in spiced or heavily fruited cakes where the margarine flavour will not be noticed. *Soft margarine* is widely used for creamed mixtures and for icings, and it gives a soft, light texture, while the flavour may be masked by chocolate, coffee, etc. Soft margarine is not suitable for pastry, but block margarine is good on its own, or it may be mixed with *lard*, which gives a flaky texture to pastry. Lard is also often used for doughs to be cooked on a griddle, giving a light, flaky texture. If animal fats are not used, *vegetable margarine* may be substituted.

Eggs

Eggs give volume, colour and flavour to cakes and any type may be used, but richly coloured, free-range ones can give a very yellow result. The standard egg for cake recipes weighs 50 g (2 oz) and a size 3 egg is suitable. If larger or smaller eggs are used, or if duck or goose eggs are available, it is wise to weigh them to get the correct equivalent for the chosen recipe.

Liquids

Milk is the main liquid used in baking. This may be liquid or reconstituted powder, and those types which are low in fat may be used. *Buttermilk* is often available and gives a beautiful texture to scones, griddlecakes and soda breads. *Sour milk* may be used instead; to obtain this, lightly sour fresh milk with a little lemon juice. It is now becoming popular to use *natural yoghurt* in cakes; the flavour is not detectable but the texture is soft and moist. For some cakes, *cider* or *stout* forms the liquid and gives a rich flavour and light texture.

Dried Fruit

Until quite recently, it was necessary to wash dried fruit and dry it before use in a cake. Today's fruit, whether sold loose or in packets, is very clean and fresh, but it is wise to inspect the fruit carefully and pick out any pieces of stem or the occasional stone. *Peel* may be bought ready-chopped, which is convenient, but it may be bought in a piece if an individual flavour such as orange or citron is required. This peel is usually a little harder, and the flavour is more pronounced.

Flavourings

It is important to use pure, high-quality flavourings in baking, because a cheap flavouring will ruin a good cake. *Ground spices* should be very fresh, and as they stale quickly, they should be bought in small quantities. *Essences, extracts* and *flavoured oils* should be pure and strong, and only a few drops are needed. *Vanilla* flavour is most easily introduced by burying a vanilla pod in a container of caster sugar, which takes on the pure scent of vanilla beans. *Coffee essence* is often used, but it is sweet, and many people prefer to use strong, fresh coffee, heated and reduced until syrupy. *Coffee powder* or *granules* may be used but should be mixed with a little hot water first. *Plain chocolate* or *cocoa* gives a clean, pure flavour; 'flavoured cooking chocolate' is fatty and has a poor flavour. *Baker's chocolate* is sometimes available, but it is very expensive; if you do use it, make sure that it is totally unsweetened, and follow the packet instructions carefully.

Nutrition

Healthy eating need not be a penance. The Ancient Greeks had a motto 'Moderation in all things', which is worth considering when modern diets are being planned. A healthy and happy person can enjoy one of life's pleasures – eating – without being fanatical, if a little thought and care are used in selecting raw materials, and if there is some restraint in eating favourite foods. It is not wise, for instance, to reject fats completely, or to over-indulge in bran and other bulky fibre foods, because a diet can quickly become unbalanced and result in a loss of valuable nutrients. It is just as unwise to eat too much sugar or animal fat, and the sensible cook will protect the family from disaster by substituting healthier ingredients and restricting the size of portions when the occasion arises.

A varied, well-balanced diet is therefore essential to good health, and attention should be paid to foods not fads. Food is essential for energy to work and keep warm, to help growth and to repair body tissue, and to help control body functions.

Everyone needs a balanced diet containing proteins, fats and carbohydrates, each of which performs a valuable function in body maintenance, as well as minerals and vitamins.

Proteins

Protein is necessary for growth, and it is particularly important for children to eat enough to develop healthy bones, muscles, skin and blood. Adults need protein for the replacement of old tissue. Proteins are composed of amino acids, and there are 28 of these commonly found in foods, 8 being essential to adults and 10 to growing children. These essential amino acids can only be supplied by the foods we eat and animal protein usually contains all of them.

Vegetable proteins are normally deficient in some essential amino-acids, but if animal foods are excluded from the diet, carefully combining protein from different vegetable sources, such as grains, nuts and legumes, will ensure an adequate protein intake.

Fats

A body must have fat to provide energy and to form body fat for warmth and protection. Fats are digested more slowly than carbohydrates and so do not provide such a quick source of energy; this is useful in maintaining a constant rather than a fluctuating energy level. Fats are an essential nutrient and a very concentrated form of energy, but because of this it is easy to eat too much of them, leading to a gain in weight. In fact, too much fat in the diet is thought to be a major cause of obesity, which has important effects on overall health, most seriously on the risk of developing cardiovascular diseases.

Cholesterol is a fat-like substance essential to the metabolism. However, the body normally produces enough cholesterol for its own needs; indeed, too high a level of cholesterol in the blood is thought to increase the risk of heart disease in people who are susceptible to the laying down of cholesterol deposits in the arteries.

A high level of saturated fats – such as butter, whole milk, cream and cheese – in the diet is likely to raise the blood cholesterol level, and it is wise to take as large a proportion as possible of your fat intake from fats high in polyunsaturates, such as some vegetable margarines and oils like safflower, sunflower and soya. Remember, though, if slimming is the aim, that all types of fat have the same calorific value.

Carbohydrates

While fats, proteins and carbohydrates all provide energy, the proteins are also needed for growth and maintenance of body tissue. It is therefore important, particularly for children, to have an adequate intake of carbohydrates to ensure that proteins are used primarily for body building rather than for energy production. There are three types of carbohydrates.

Sugars (found mainly in all types of sugar, honey, jam, syrup, dried fruit and fresh fruit, especially bananas) provide a quick, valuable source of energy, particularly for children, but over-indulgence can result in overweight if this energy is not burnt up.

Foods high in *starches* are often less fattening than high sugar foods because they are high in dietary fibre. They include flour, cereals, bread, pasta, rice, potatoes, starchy vegetables and pulses, which are also sources of protein, minerals and vitamins.

The third type of carbohydrate is *cellulose* or dietary fibre, which is indigestible by the human body but which forms important roughage in the diet. Cellulose forms the cell walls of fruit and vegetables and is also found in unrefined cereals and nuts.

The fibrous part of plant foods is a carbohydrate which was once thought to be useless because it cannot be digested. It used to be known as roughage, but is now usually described as dietary fibre, and is, in fact, essential to the health of the digestive system; with adequate intake, waste products are quickly and efficiently eliminated from the body. Many diet-related diseases can be guarded against if we eat enough fibre.

Fibre is particularly important to slimmers, because it provides satisfying bulk without extra calories. Fresh fruit and vegetables, including their skins, provide fibre, but wholemeal bread, and the flour and cereals which go into home-baked dishes are a really excellent source which will be popular and acceptable to everybody.

Vitamins and Minerals

Vitamins and minerals are vital to the body, but are present in only very small quantities in food. They help to use the other nutrients in food and protect the body from illness, and a good mixed diet will provide all the necessary vitamins and minerals.

Vitamin A (found in butter, margarine, cheese, eggs, herrings, sardines, liver, almonds and peanuts) is essential for growth, keeps skin and eyes healthy and helps sight, as well as keeping the throat and breathing passages in good order. The Vitamin B group (found in yeast extract, wholemeal bread, wheatgerm, cereals, liver, beef, pork, bacon, cheese, fish and pulses) is essential for metabolic processes, especially obtaining energy from carbohydrates. These vitamins cannot be stored in the body and must be taken every day. Vitamin C (from fresh fruit and vegetables) cannot be stored in the body and a daily intake is essential for the growth and repair of tissues and for resistance to infection. Vitamin D (which comes from milk, butter, margarine, eggs, liver and oily fish) is important for the absorption and laying down of calcium in the bones, and is particularly important for children and expectant mothers.

The five most important minerals are calcium, iron, sodium, potassium and iodine. Calcium (found in milk, cheese, bread and sardines) is needed for the development of bones, teeth, muscles and blood, and for continued growth. Iron (found in liver, kidney, beef, green vegetables, whole grain cereals, dried fruit and cocoa powder) is needed for the proper functioning of the blood. Sodium (found in all products and foods containing salt, including bacon, ham, seafood, cheese and most processed foods) is necessary for the normal balance of body fluids. The average diet is very high in sodium and since this may be a contributory factor in high blood pressure, most people should try to restrict their intake. Potassium (from wheatgerm, bran, nuts and seeds and whole grains) complements sodium in its functions and also helps to regulate the level of sodium in the system. Iodine (from watercress, spinach and seafood) is needed for the production of thyroid hormones, which control growth and development.

Calorie Counting

It is interesting to see how surplus calories occur in the diet. A calorie is a measure of the energy generated by food, and, if more calories are eaten than are expended in movement and metabolism, the surplus is laid down in excess fat. Energy-rich foods consist of high fat foods, and also those containing protein and refined carbohydrates, especially sugars. The average man needs 2500 to 3500 Calories a day for weight maintenance; the average woman needs 1800 to 2500 Calories a day. (One Calorie, or kilocalorie, equals 1000 calories; when measuring the energy content of food in everyday terms, the larger unit, with the capital 'C', is usually used for convenience.) A daily Calorie allowance for weight loss is 1400 to 1600 for men and 1000 to 1200 for women.

It's easy to see from a chart which foods are highest in calories, but it is most important to remember that a calorie-controlled diet must still be a balanced one. Don't cut out the sources of any nutrient completely, or ill-health will result; instead, try to eat a variety of foods without over-indulgence in any one kind. Keep an eye on how many fatty and sugary foods you are eating, as these are the most usual cause of overweight, but you should find that if you are paying attention to the quality and balance of your diet, your weight will stabilise at the correct level and you should not gain weight in future.

The Importance of Home Baking

Home baking can play an important part in presenting a balanced diet to a family. The essential cereals, flours, fats, dried fruits, nuts and iron-rich chocolate and cocoa can be incorporated into dishes which are palatable but healthy. The individual cook is free to experiment, perhaps pairing a wholewheat pastry with fruit or meat, adding cheese to bread or biscuits, or substituting black treacle for syrup. Good bread is almost essential to a healthy diet, but cake is not necessarily evil, and to quote an old song 'a little of what you fancy does you good'. We only need to remember a modern ending: 'as long as you don't indulge too often'.

Baking Equipment

It is not necessary to buy large quantities of special and expensive equipment to be a successful baker, because, for centuries, cooks managed with a bowl, a clay container or well-worn tin and an uncertain oven. Originally, cakes were beaten with bare hands or a wooden spoon or twig whisk, but now kitchen shops and departments are full of exciting equipment and it is very difficult to know what to choose.

Basic Essentials

A large mixing bowl is the first essential for baking, so that air can be incorporated into a mixture without spillage. A wooden spoon is sufficient for beating, although some people like to use a large, strong fork. For whisking, a balloon whisk or rotary whisk may be used. For speed and efficiency, a variety of electrical equipment is available (see overleaf). As well as the basic large mixing bowl, small bowls may be needed for preliminary beating of eggs or small quantities of ingredients measured in advance.

Accurate measuring scales are also essential, calibrated in either metric or imperial units. The weighing bowl must be large enough to hold a considerable volume of flour or other light ingredients. A measuring jug is useful for measuring liquid ingredients. A tablespoon and a teaspoon are needed all the time for measuring small quantities; for total accuracy, a set of measuring spoons may be bought cheaply.

For pastry making, a sharp knife is useful for trimming edges. Metal cutters are necessary for biscuit making. (They are better than plastic ones, which do not have a good cutting edge.) A wooden rolling pin is best; buy a long one without handles, which impede the even pressure necessary for pastry and biscuits.

A sieve is necessary for incorporating air into flour, and for smoothing icing sugar. One with a nylon mesh is better than a metal one which can discolour sugar and which is not easy to keep dry. A wire cake rack is the final essential, as cakes must be cooled on something which allows air to circulate, so that the warm air is dispersed and the cake remains light. In an emergency, the rack of a grill pan may be used.

Tins

The correct tin makes all the difference between a successful cake and a failure. Tins should be strong and thick, so that they do not buckle after use or dent when stored. They may be coated with a non-stick surface, although it may be necessary to line the tins if the surface becomes damaged.

Baking sheets should be thick and heavy, and preferably without an edge on three sides, so that flan rings may be slipped off and biscuits removed easily. For most biscuit recipes, two tins will be needed to avoid crowding. A shallow rectangular *swiss roll tin* is useful for that type of cake, but may also be used for biscuits. *Rectangular* and *square tins* need a depth of no less than 5 cm (2 in), but ordinary roasting tins may be used for tray fruit cakes and gingerbreads. *Deep, round tins* are traditional for many cakes and these should be at least 7.5 cm (3 in) deep. Those with 15 cm (6 in), 17.5 cm (7 in) and 20 cm (8 in) diameters are used most often, and if they have removable bases, the tins will be more useful as cakes may be more easily turned out. *Sponge sandwich tins* are about 3.75–5 cm (1½–2 in) deep, the slightly deeper ones being the most useful as they prevent the mixture overflowing and forming a hard rim. The best sizes are 17.5 cm (7 in) and 20 cm (8 in), although a shallow 22.5 cm (9 in) tin is useful for gâteaux when a thin sheet of sponge is needed. These tins should be bought in pairs, but it is worth having four sandwich tins as it is very easy to make a double quantity of the mixture, so that you fill the oven and can freeze one of the cakes later.

Paper

A selection of baking papers is most useful for baking. *Greaseproof paper* is used for lining tins, but non-stick *baking parchment* is excellent for slightly sticky mixtures like meringues or brandy snaps. Ready-cut discs and lining strips of baking parchment are available, and are a tremendous help to the busy cook, or to anyone who wishes to bake large quantities. *Large paper cases* which slip into round cake tins may also be bought and are useful if cakes are to be sold: small paper cases may be used for individual small cakes.

Mixers, Food Processors and Electric Whisks

Electrical gadgets speed up preparation, and are particularly useful for making quantities of baked goods. The *hand-held electric whisk* is not expensive and is ideal for whisking eggs or egg whites, whipping cream, and whipping mixtures over heat. Most electric whisks will cope with a single cake mixture, but are not strong enough to cope with double quantities or heavy fruit cakes.

Electric mixers are excellent for larger quantities of pastry, bread or cake mixtures. The attachments include a balloon whisk for egg whites and cream, a heavy beater for cake mixtures, and a dough hook (optional) for kneading yeast dough. Some *electric blenders* are attachments for mixers; others are free-standing. They are useful for the additional chores such as chopping nuts, chocolate or cheese, and making breadcrumbs and batters.

Food processors are the latest aid to home-bakers. The processor is very good for making sponge cakes and other cakes which use soft margarine and an all-in-one creaming method. It is also good for making creamy-light icings, and for preparing pastry and bread dough. The blade of the processor will also chop nuts, chocolate or fruit for adding to mixtures, and will rapidly produce cake or biscuit crumbs.

Ovens

Gas or electric cookers, or enclosed stoves fuelled by oil, gas, electricity or solid fuel will all produce good baking results. The most important thing to remember is the control of temperature, and ovens can become very inaccurate over the years. For this reason, an *oven thermometer* is a worthwhile investment to check accuracy, and even to see if there is a variation according to the position of shelves in the oven.

If using fan or convection ovens, be sure to read the manufacturer's instructions carefully for advice on baking in them, as some small adjustment may be necessary to temperature.

Basic methods
of
oven baking

W

hichever recipes are chosen, it is important to organise a baking session intelligently, because it is expensive to use an oven for just one cake. In the days when cooks had to rely on an oven fuelled with wood, bread was baked first in the newly hot oven. Then came the cakes or biscuits which needed a moderate oven, and finally the more delicate items would be baked in the dying oven as it cooled. Farm wives even used to cook an oven-bottom cake overnight to take advantage of the last vestiges of heat.

Today, our ovens are carefully controlled, but it still makes sense to prepare bread and yeast bakes or scones first, since these need the hottest oven. While these are baking, cake mixtures may be prepared, ready for when the oven temperature is lowered. Biscuit mixtures do not suffer from standing a while and can be ready for the lower temperatures, and finally items like meringues can be dried out in the cooling oven. Of course, not everybody wants to indulge in a marathon bake-in, but it still makes sense to use the heat from weekend cooking operations, for instance, baking a fruit pie along with the Sunday roast, and perhaps some extra pastry items to fill lunch-boxes during the week, and then some cakes or biscuits can go into a cooler oven immediately afterwards and be ready for that family occasion, Sunday tea. Since most baked goods store well in the refrigerator, freezer or airtight tins, it is practical to use the oven for this small batch-bake which will supply the needs of a household for a few days.

If preparing a number of recipes, try to choose those which need the same oven temperature, or only have a slight variation. The top of the traditional oven is slightly hotter, so it is possible to bake a variety of recipes at one time. It is, however, important to take timing into consideration too, since biscuits and scones need only short baking and should not be paired with cakes which need much longer and will sink and spoil if the oven is opened during their cooking time.

Preparing a Recipe

However many recipes are being prepared at one time, it is vital to read them through carefully first to make sure that all the ingredients are to hand. All ingredients and utensils should then be assembled, as there is nothing more tiring than endless trips across a kitchen for forgotten items.

Inexperienced cooks may find it wise to note any special points about a recipe on a piece of paper, or to check off ingredients as they are incorporated. A kitchen timer also aids the memory, but if two or three items are being baked at the same time, it may also be necessary to note down the times at which they need to be taken out of the oven. Often, experienced cooks make use of a piece of paper to make a worksheet, so that they can, for instance, grease and line all their tins together, or prepare all the fruit for a batch of recipes to save time and energy.

Using Electrical Equipment

The modern cook can take advantage of hand-held electric whisks, blenders, mixers and food processors which speed up work considerably and prevent too much strain on the arms and back. These pieces of equipment encourage the baking of batches of food (such as preparing two or three lots of pastry at a time, or two sponge cakes instead of one) without increasing the burden of washing-up. The manufacturer's instructions should always be consulted, however, until you are thoroughly used to a machine, as it is easy to overmix or overbeat ingredients and therefore get poor results.

Bread

Baking with yeast is not complicated if a few simple facts are understood, and once the art is mastered, this is a thoroughly satisfying branch of cookery. Anyone can tackle the recipes on pages 38–48, but it is best to begin with a simple white dough and perfect this after one or two baking sessions before going on to slightly more complicated recipes.

Yeast

Most breads are raised with yeast, although quick breads may be raised with bicarbonate of soda or even baking powder. Yeast is a living organism which is activated by warmth. Its action is retarded by a low temperature, and is finally killed off by the high temperature used in bread baking. Yeast may be fresh or dried but must be activated with liquid before use. The exception is easy-blend dried yeast, which needs a different technique (page 9), and the manufacturer's instructions must be followed for this type.

Fresh yeast should be mixed into the warm liquid from the recipe and left to froth. A little sugar acts as food for the yeast and encourages frothing, but too much kills the yeast cells and causes the 'yeasty' flavour associated with badly made bread. Salt is essential to give flavour to yeasted breads, but it prevents the yeast fermenting quickly and too much of it will kill the yeast, so it should be added to the dry ingredients, *not* to the liquid.

Dried yeast should be sprinkled over the *warm* liquid. A teaspoon of sugar will encourage quick frothing. The liquid should be left in a warm place for at least 10 minutes, until the yeast is frothing strongly (up to 20 minutes may be needed).

The quantity of yeast needed to raise dough varies according to the type of flour used and the dough being made. White flour needs less yeast than wholemeal flour, while enriched doughs need extra yeast because its growth is retarded by additional fat, sugar, eggs and fruit. The recipes in this book give the exact quantities required, and it should be noted that the weight of dried yeast required is half that of fresh yeast.

Mix fresh yeast with warm water and leave it to froth.

Liquid

Yeast doughs may be prepared with water, milk, or a mixture of the two. Milk adds extra food value, helps to strengthen dough and improves the keeping quality of the baked product. The quantity required depends on the flour and type of recipe, as white flour absorbs less liquid than wholemeal flour; generally, 300 ml (½ pint) liquid is needed for every 500 g (1 lb) strong bread flour. All the liquid should be added at once to the dry ingredients, and extra flour should not be worked in unless it is absolutely necessary because the dough is too soft to handle easily, and this is not always apparent until the dough has been well kneaded.

The temperature of the liquid should be 44°C (110°F) to start the yeast working. As a rough guide, two parts of cold water to one part of boiling water will give the correct temperature.

Fat

Fat should not be omitted from yeast doughs as it helps to enrich them, increases loaf volume, improves the softness and colour of the crumb, and delays staling. When the fat is melted before use, it should be cooled but still liquid when added to the other ingredients. Butter, margarine or lard may be used.

Flour

The type of flour used may vary according to the final result which is desired (page 8), but for yeast baking, it must always be made from hard wheat and is known as strong or bread flour. This flour absorbs more liquid than soft (cake) flour, and develops gluten quickly, so that, with kneading, a firm, elastic dough is obtained. It gives a larger volume and lighter texture than would be obtained using soft flour.

Wholemeal flour gives variety in colour and flavour to bread, as well as a slightly chewy texture. The flour gives a more limited rise and closer texture than white flour. Rye flour produces a slightly tough bread with a subtle sour taste which is good with meat, fish or cheese. Barley flour and oatmeal are not suitable for yeast-raised breads, but they work well with other raising agents for a loaf which needs to be eaten freshly baked.

Preparing Yeast Dough

Basic yeast dough is made by adding the warm yeasted liquid to the dry ingredients and forming the mixture into a soft but firm ball. This then has to be kneaded to strengthen and develop the dough and to give a good rise and even texture. A slightly different method is used for cake-breads, with a little flour added to the liquid to make a spongy batter before the rest of the dry ingredients are worked in.

Mixing the Dough

The dry ingredients should be placed in a warm bowl which will encourage the development of the dough when the liquid has been added. When the yeast liquid is frothing strongly, it must be added all at once and the dough formed with the hands (or mixer hook or food processor) until all the dry ingredients have been incorporated.

Kneading

As soon as the dough has formed, it must be kneaded; this takes about 10 minutes by hand, but only a couple of

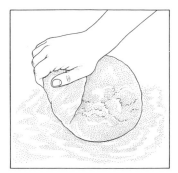

Knead dough by hand on a lightly floured surface.

Prove dough in a lightly oiled, covered bowl.

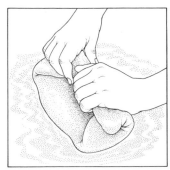

Shape dough to fit a loaf tin by rolling it up gently.

Prove the shaped dough in the tin.

minutes with a mixer or food processor. To knead by hand, put the dough on a very lightly floured surface and form into a neat ball. Keep the fingers together and fold the dough towards the body. Push down and away with the palm of the hand. Give the dough a quarter turn and repeat the kneading, using a rocking rhythm, and employing both hands or just one hand. Continue until the dough is no longer sticky, is elastic and firm and has a satiny surface.

Rising or Proving
Yeast doughs must be allowed to rise at least once before baking so that the yeast has time to work right through the dough. Dough will form a skin during the process and this must be prevented (except for French Flutes) during rising. After kneading, put the ball of dough into a lightly oiled bowl and cover with a clean, damp cloth, or put the dough into a lightly oiled polythene bag, tied loosely at the top so that there is space for the dough to rise.

A warm place gives a quick rise in about 45–60 minutes; the dough will take 1½–2 hours at room temperature. The dough may be put to rise in a cold room for 8–12 hours, or in a refrigerator, where it will take 24 hours. A slow rise controls the yeast growth and the dough rises gradually to produce an excellent finished product. This can be useful if a dough is prepared in the evening ready for morning baking. If the dough has been left to rise in a cold place, it is wise to allow it to come to room temperature before baking. Richer doughs take longer to rise than plain ones and benefit from a slow, cool rise.

After the first rising, the dough should be knocked back with the knuckles to remove air bubbles and then kneaded again to make the dough firm for shaping (this will take about 3 minutes by hand). After this, the dough may be shaped freehand or put into tins. It should then be covered as for the first rising and left to rise or prove again until it has doubled in size or is just filling the tins.

Shaping and Baking
Dough must never be torn apart, as this spoils the action of the dough. It should be cut with a knife, and if small items such as rolls are being made, the dough should be weighed so that the pieces are even in size. Shape the dough by forming into balls, or plaiting, and put freehand shapes on greased baking sheets before proving. If filling tins, make sure that they are well greased and that the dough is fitted in neatly by being shaped into an oval before it is put into the tins. Try to avoid creases and folds as these will show up in the finished loaves. After proving and/or baking, a variety of finishes may be applied to the bread (page 38).

Yeast doughs must be baked in a hot oven to kill off the action of the fermenting yeast. Plain breads are baked in a very hot oven (Gas Mark 8/230°C/450°F). Enriched doughs are baked in a cooler oven (Gas Mark 5–6/190–200°C/375–400°F). Loaves in tins shrink slightly from the sides of the tins when cooked, and all bread is cooked when golden brown in colour. It will sound hollow when tapped underneath, and if not quite cooked, may be returned to the oven without the tin for a further 5 minutes. Cool bread on a wire rack before use.

Cakes

Cakes must be made with fresh, high-quality ingredients, or they will taste stale, but apart from this, the cake-making rules present no problems. All ingredients, including eggs and fats, should be at room temperature before use. The oven should be switched on before the cake mixture is prepared so that the correct temperature is achieved by the time the mixture is in tins.

Rubbed-in mixtures are used for plainer cakes. The dry ingredients such as flour, salt and spices should be sieved into a bowl. The fat should then be added and worked with a knife or the tips of the fingers until the mixture resembles fine breadcrumbs. Other dry ingredients, such as sugar and fruit, are then added, followed by the liquids like milk and eggs. A final beating distributes the ingredients before the mixture is put into the tin.

Creamed mixtures are for lighter cakes such as sponge sandwiches. The fat should be soft but not melted and it can then easily be beaten with a wooden spoon or a mixer. Caster sugar must be used as it dissolves quickly in the fat.

Use the fingertips to combine fat and flour for a rubbed-in mixture.

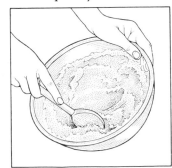

Beat the fat and sugar together until light and fluffy for a creamed cake mixture.

When it is added, the mixture must be beaten hard until light and fluffy and pale in colour. Eggs should be lightly beaten first to distribute the yolks and whites, and the flour should be sieved. The egg mixture and flour should be added alternately in small amounts to prevent curdling. Fold them in lightly and finally beat well. When the milk or other liquid, remaining flour and other ingredients are added, the mixture is best stirred and folded lightly, without further beating or the carefully added air from the initial beating will be dispersed. A modern and quick method of preparing creamed mixtures is known as the *all-in-one method*. For this, soft margarine must be used, and all the ingredients are placed in a large bowl together before being beaten vigorously for 2–3 minutes until light and creamy. (This method is also used for cakes in the food processor.)

The melting method is used mainly for gingerbreads. The fat and semi-liquid sweetening agent, such as black treacle or golden syrup, are heated together gently until just melted and amalgamated before they are added to the dry ingredients and beaten well. The melting method is also used for 'boiled' fruit cakes in which the fat, sugar, liquid and dried fruit are simmered together until the fruit is plump, and then cooled before they are added to the dry ingredients. This results in a soft, moist cake.

Whisked mixtures may be prepared by whisking egg yolks or whole eggs with sugar as the first stage of cake preparation. The result should be very light and fluffy and extremely pale. If a mixture has to be beaten over hot water, the bowl must not touch the water or the eggs will set and will not mix well with the sugar or retain air. If egg whites are to be whisked separately as part of a recipe, the eggs must be separated very carefully so that no trace of yolk is left in the white, as this will lessen the volume of the whisked whites and alter the texture of the result. The bowl for whisking whites must also be completely dry and free of grease.

Folding in Ingredients

When ingredients have to be folded into a mixture, this should be done with a knife or metal spoon, using a sharp, clean action like cutting a cake, then lifting to bring the heavier substances from the bottom of the bowl in a figure-of-eight motion. Lighter mixtures should be folded into heavier ones, and flour into creamed mixtures, so that air is not pressed out. If folding in whisked egg whites, fold in just a spoonful or two first to lighten the basic mixture and it will then be easier to fold in the rest of the whites and achieve an even-coloured and even-textured mixture.

Consistency

The experienced cook has learned to recognise the consistency of a mixture which will affect the finished texture after baking. A *soft dropping consistency* means that the mixture is too stiff to pour, but will drop from a spoon without being shaken. *Stiff dropping consistency* means that the mixture is too soft and sticky to handle, but is stiff enough to keep its shape when shaken from a spoon.

Preparing Tins

It is most important to use the size of tin specified in the recipe, as the volume of a mixture affects the cooking time,

To make a cake mixture using the melting method, heat the fat and golden syrup before beating in the dry ingredients.

Line the base of a cake tin with greaseproof paper to ease removal.

and a mixture which is placed in a small, high tin will take longer to cook through than the same quantity in a larger, shallower tin. Tins should be well greased with butter, lard or oil, remembering that these can flavour the finished mixture: it would be a mistake to grease a tin for a delicate butter flavoured cake with lard or a strongly flavoured oil. Margarine may contain non-fat liquid which will make a cake mixture stick in the tin if it is used as the greasing agent.

For sponge cake mixtures, the greased tin may be lightly dusted with flour to give a smooth surface, or with a mixture of flour and caster sugar to give a lightly crusted surface. For safety, it is a good idea to base-line the tins with a circle of greaseproof paper or baking parchment. Cakes which need longer cooking should be baked in fully lined tins with a side lining of greaseproof paper or baking parchment.

Baking and Testing

The specified temperature must be used for baking cakes, and if a number of cake recipes seem to have the 'wrong' timing, this is probably because the cook's own oven is not running at the temperature indicated on the control switch. Ovens are not always accurate when installed, and the temperatures can vary after years of use, so it is worth checking the temperatures with an oven thermometer from time to time.

A cooked cake should have risen well and evenly over the whole surface, and should be a golden colour, and firm and springy when pressed lightly. Most cakes will shrink slightly from the edge of the tin when cooled. Rich fruit cakes make a slight singing noise while baking, and this should cease when the cake is ready. If the cake does not appear quite cooked in the specified time, test it by inserting a thin skewer or knife in the centre: it will come out dry and clean if the cake is ready. The oven should not be opened until the cooking time is completed, or the cake may sink.

Cooling

It is wise to leave a cake in its tin for a minute or two to firm up before turning it out, or it may break when the supporting tin is removed. Rich fruit cakes may be left to cool for an hour before turning out, and tray-bakes can be left to cool in the tins and iced while still in place. Cakes should be turned out on to a wire cake rack to finish cooling, and should not be stored until completely cold.

Pastry

Good pastry is not difficult to make, but a little extra care will produce delicious results. There are a number of different types of pastry but they fall into two main categories. *Short pastry* is made by rubbing fat into flour which breaks up the gluten. Each flour grain is covered and the fat keeps the grains separate when the liquid is added. *Flaky and puff pastry* must rise in layers of thin flakes and this is achieved by adding the fat in pieces instead of rubbing in, and then by repeated folding and rolling so that layers of dough are covered by layers of fat.

Ingredients and Proportions

Plain flour is recommended for pastry, and although self-raising flour may be used, the result is slightly spongy. Strong bread flour is recommended for flaky pastries. Flour should be fresh, or it will give a stale flavour to the pastry.

The fat used may be hard margarine, butter or lard (which gives a flaky texture), or a specially formulated cooking fat. For everyday use, a mixture of hard margarine and lard is satisfactory. The proportion of fat to flour should be as stated in the recipe. Too little fat makes pastry hard, and too much makes pastry unmanageable and very short and crumbly. An average recipe allows one part of fat to two parts of flour for shortcrust pastry; flaky pastries require a higher proportion of fat to be incorporated in the folding and rolling processes.

Preparing Pastry

The ingredients and the finished dough for pastry should be cold for best results, and pastry should be handled as little as possible so that the heat of the hands does not melt the fat. The fat should be soft enough to rub in easily with the fingers and thumbs, or a knife, until the mixture looks like fine breadcrumbs. If the mixture is over-rubbed, the pastry will break when rolled out. If the pieces of fat and flour begin to grow bigger again instead of smaller, the mixture is being over-rubbed. Only a little water is needed to complete the pastry mixture, and this should be ice-cold. Usually about 2 tablespoons of water is enough for 250 g (8 oz) flour, and it should be added all at once. The dough should be firm but not sticky. If it is too dry, the pastry will crack. If using a mixer or food processor, stop the machine as soon as a ball of dough is formed.

Pastry should be rolled out on a very lightly floured marble slab or other flat surface and it should not be handled or rolled too much. It should be shaped into a circle, square or rectangle (according to the end use) before rolling evenly. Pastry must not be *stretched* on to a pie or into a tin, or it will shrink away from the edge during cooking. It is better to roll a piece larger than required and trim the pastry when it is in place.

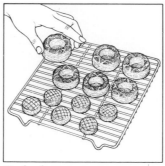

Cool vol-au-vent cases on a wire rack to keep the pastry crisp.

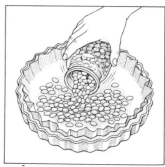

Bake an empty pastry case 'blind'.

Baking

Pastry requires a hot oven, with the flaky varieties needing the highest setting (see recipes on pages 66–68). If a pie has an undercrust, or a tart or flan is being baked, the container should be placed on a baking sheet which has already been heated in the oven, and this will help to cook the base quickly so that it remains crisp. When lining a flan ring, pie plate or tartlet tins, the pastry should be pressed firmly into the base to expel air, or the air will expand in the heat of the oven and push the pastry up through the filling. If cooked pastry is removed from the tins while hot (e.g. tartlets, vol-au-vent cases), the items should be cooled on a wire rack so that the steam escapes and the pastry remains crisp.

Baking Blind

Sometimes pastry cases need to be partially or completely baked before they are filled, and this is known as 'baking blind'. The easiest way to get good results is to prick the base of the pastry lightly with a fork and line it with foil. Alternatively, an unpricked pastry base may be lined with greaseproof paper, which must then be filled with baking beans or rice to prevent the pastry rising during cooking. After baking for the time specified in the recipe (usually 15–20 minutes), the covering should be removed and the pastry baked for a further 5 minutes to ensure crispness.

Top Italian Torrone (p. 26); *Bottom*
Drop Scones (p. 20)

Baking without an oven

*U*ntil the late eighteenth century, few houses had ovens, and cooks had to prepare all their food over an open fire on a hearth at the side of the kitchen or living room. The first breads, cakes and pastries were prepared on a large stone set in a hot fire. Batters or doughs were placed on the hot surface to cook and seal one side, then flipped over to finish cooking.

From the early bakestone, the griddle developed in the form of a thick, flat iron plate on a very long handle or on a loop which could be suspended over the flames. Griddles are still obtainable, but a heavy frying pan may be used instead.

The griddle or pan should be heated to a moderate temperature on top of a gas, electric or solid fuel cooker. To test the heat, sprinkle on a little flour: if it browns instantly, the surface is too hot; if it colours slowly, the surface is at the correct temperature.

The surface of the pan or griddle should be lightly floured for dough (giving a dry, floury surface), but greased for batter. A little oil or lard may be used, and the surface should never be washed but rubbed with a little salt when hot, and then wiped with clean paper or a piece of cloth. This gives a surface on which food will not burn.

If a griddle or heavy frying pan is not available, these recipes may be adapted for the oven. Baking sheets should be floured or greased according to the recipe and the cakes placed on top. The best oven temperature is Gas Mark 7/ 220°C/325°F.

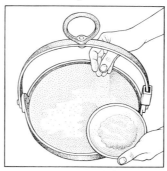

Prepare a griddle with flour before baking doughs.

Use a palette knife to lift and turn half-cooked scones on the griddle.

Drop Scones

These scones are like small, thick, soft pancakes, and they are at their best spread with butter and eaten while still warm.

Makes 18 scones
Time Preparation 10 minutes, Baking 15 minutes

Ingredients

250 g (8 oz) self-raising flour	300 ml (½ pint) milk
50 g (2 oz) caster sugar	1 teaspoon cream of tartar
2 eggs	

Method
Sieve the flour into a bowl and stir in the sugar. Beat the eggs and milk together. Add to the flour with the cream of tartar and beat well to make a thick, creamy batter.

Grease a griddle or thick frying pan lightly and warm to moderate heat. Pour on tablespoonfuls of batter, allowing each one room to spread. Cook over a moderate heat until bubbles begin to form and burst on the top of the scones. Lift the scones, turn them carefully with a palette knife, and cook until the second side is golden.

Lift the scones on to a wire rack and wrap in a clean cloth so that they remain soft. Continue cooking until all the batter has been used. Spread with butter just before serving.

Potato Scones

These light scones may be made with leftover potatoes and are delicious with butter, or with the breakfast bacon.

Makes 12 scones
Time Preparation 20 minutes, Baking 8 minutes

Ingredients
250 g (8 oz) potatoes, peeled
50 g (2 oz) butter
125 g (4 oz) plain flour
½ teaspoon baking powder
¼ teaspoon salt

Method
Boil the potatoes in lightly salted water until tender. Drain very well and mash with the butter. Sieve together the flour, baking powder and salt and add to the potatoes. Knead well to make a soft but firm dough.

Roll out the dough to a thickness of 1.25 cm (½ in) on a lightly floured board. Cut into 7.5 cm (3 in) rounds with a plain cutter, and prick once or twice with a fork. Cook the scones on a hot, lightly floured griddle for 4 minutes on each side. Serve hot with butter.

Baking
Bake on a lightly floured baking sheet at Gas Mark 7/ 220°C/425°F for 10 minutes.

Griddle Scones

Simple scones cooked quickly on top of the stove, these are delicious with butter, or with jam and cream.

Makes 12–15 scones
Time Preparation 10 minutes, Baking 8 minutes

Ingredients
250 g (8 oz) self-raising flour
¼ teaspoon salt
40 g (1½ oz) butter,
    cut into pieces
25 g (1 oz) sugar
approx. 150 ml (¼ pint)
    milk

Method
Sieve the flour and salt into a bowl. Rub in the butter until the mixture is like fine breadcrumbs. Stir in the sugar until evenly mixed. Add sufficient milk to bind and mix to a soft, firm dough.

Knead well and roll out the dough to a thickness of 1.25 cm (½ in) on a lightly floured board. Cut into 5 cm (2 in) rounds with a plain cutter.

Cook on a hot, floured griddle for 4 minutes. Turn the scones carefully, and continue cooking for 4 minutes. Serve freshly made.

Top Fruit Biscuit Cake (p. 24); *Bottom* Spiced Raisin Flan (p. 25)

Oatcakes

Oatcakes keep well in a tin and they are delicious with cheese or with the breakfast marmalade.

Makes 16 oatcakes
Time Preparation 15 minutes, Baking 10 minutes, Drying 4 hours

Ingredients
125 g (4 oz) medium
    oatmeal
25 g (1 oz) plain flour
25 g (1 oz) butter,
    cut into very small pieces
25 g (1 oz) lard,
    cut into very small pieces
15 g (½ oz) sugar
pinch of salt
pinch of bicarbonate of soda
2–3 tablespoons boiling
    water

Method
Stir the oatmeal and flour together in a bowl. Stir the small pieces of butter and lard into the dry ingredients. Sprinkle in the sugar, salt and bicarbonate of soda. Add the boiling water, and knead the mixture until firm.

Sprinkle a little extra oatmeal on a board. Divide the dough into quarters. Roll out one piece into a thin round and divide it into four triangles. Repeat with each quarter of dough.

Dust a griddle or thick frying pan lightly with flour. Put on half the oatcakes and cook over moderate heat for 7 minutes. Turn the oatcakes over and continue cooking for 3 minutes. Repeat with the remaining oatcakes.

Put a wire cake rack in a roasting tin and place the oatcakes on it. Leave in a plate-warming oven or warm airing cupboard for 4 hours until crisp and dry. Store in an airtight container.

Baking
Bake on a lightly floured baking sheet at Gas Mark 8/ 230°C/450°F for 7 minutes. Turn the oatcakes and continue baking for 3 minutes. Dry as for oatcakes cooked on a griddle.

22 *Top left* Oatcakes (p. 21); *Top right* Griddle Scones (p. 21); *Bottom left* Singin' Hinny (p. 24); *Bottom right* Teisen Lap (p. 24)

Teisen Lap

This cake from Wales is nicest if made with sour milk or buttermilk, but ordinary milk may be used.

Makes 1 cake
Time Preparation 10 minutes, Baking 30 minutes

Ingredients

250 g (8 oz) plain flour	50 g (2 oz) sugar
1 teaspoon baking powder	50 g (2 oz) mixed dried fruit
pinch of salt	2 eggs
pinch of ground nutmeg	4 tablespoons milk
50 g (2 oz) butter, cut into pieces	

Method
Sieve the flour, baking powder, salt and nutmeg into a bowl. Rub in the butter until the mixture is like fine breadcrumbs. Stir in the sugar and fruit. Beat the eggs and milk together and work into the dry ingredients to make a soft, firm dough.

Roll out the dough on a lightly floured board into a rectangle 2.5 cm (1 in) thick. Lightly flour a griddle or thick frying pan. Warm over low heat and cook the cake for 15 minutes. Turn the cake carefully and cook the other side for 15 minutes. Cut in squares and serve freshly baked.

Baking
Put into a 17.5 cm × 27.5 cm (7 in × 11 in) tin. Bake at Gas Mark 4/180°C/350°F for 40 minutes.

Singin' Hinny

This cake 'sings' as it cooks, and 'hinny' is a term of endearment in Northumberland, where the cake comes from.

Makes 1 cake
Time Preparation 10 minutes, Baking 10 minutes

Ingredients

250 g (8 oz) plain flour	50 g (2 oz) lard,
½ teaspoon baking powder	cut into pieces
½ teaspoon salt	75 g (3 oz) currants
50 g (2 oz) butter, cut into pieces	150 ml (¼ pint) milk

Method
Sieve the flour, baking powder and salt into a bowl. Rub in the butter and lard until the mixture is like fine breadcrumbs. Stir in the currants and enough milk to make a stiff dough.

Roll out the dough on a lightly floured board into a large round about 2.5 cm (1 in) thick. Prick it lightly all over with a fork.

Grease a griddle or thick frying pan lightly. Warm to moderate heat and put on the cake. Cook until the cake is lightly golden on the base. Turn it carefully and cook until the second side is golden. Turn it again and cook for 1 minute. Lift the cake on to a serving plate and split it horizontally while hot. Spread with butter and serve hot.

No-bake Cakes

THE MODERN VERSION of baking without an oven is the cake or pastry made with biscuit crumbs as a bulk ingredient and without the application of heat. Cakes and pastry cases set firmly because the biscuit crumbs are bound with fat and sugar, or some other melted ingredient such as chocolate or marshmallows which reset when cold.

Semi-sweet biscuits (e.g. McVitie's Digestives) give crumbs with the correct texture and flavour for these non-bakes. The biscuits should be broken into small pieces and may then be crushed in a good processor or electric blender. The action of the machine must be monitored carefully so that the biscuits are not reduced to powder. Alternatively, the broken biscuits may be placed in a polythene bag and then crushed with a rolling pin.

Crush broken biscuits in a polythene bag with a rolling pin.

Fruit Biscuit Cake

A delicious mixture of dried fruit, nuts and biscuits with a subtle flavour of honey, this cake is a perfect companion to a cup of coffee.

Makes 16 squares
Time Preparation 10 minutes (plus chilling time)

Ingredients

175 g (6 oz) sweet biscuits	75 g (3 oz) sultanas, chopped
50 g (2 oz) butter	
50 g (2 oz) light soft brown sugar	50 g (2 oz) seedless raisins, chopped
1 egg, beaten	50 g (2 oz) glacé cherries, chopped
1 tablespoon honey	
1 teaspoon vanilla essence	50 g (2 oz) chopped walnuts

Method
Crush the biscuits into crumbs, which should not be too fine. Melt the butter in a saucepan and remove from the heat. Beat in the sugar, egg, honey and vanilla essence.

Mix the biscuit crumbs with the honey mixture, and stir in the sultanas, raisins, cherries and walnuts. Line a 20 cm (8 in) square tin with foil. Press in the crumb mixture and chill until firm. Cut into squares and remove from the tin.

Spiced Raisin Flan

The sweet, crunchy biscuit case contrasts with a smooth, spiced filling containing plump raisins. The flan is particularly delicious served with clotted cream or ice cream.

Makes 1 × 20 cm (8 in) flan
Time Preparation 15 minutes (plus chilling time)

Ingredients

125 g (4 oz) butter	250 g (8 oz) McVitie's
25 g (1 oz) sugar	Digestive Biscuits, crushed

Filling

175 g (6 oz) seedless raisins	½ teaspoon ground
200 ml (7 fl oz) water	cinnamon
1 tablespoon cornflour	75 g (3 oz) dark soft brown
½ teaspoon ground cloves	sugar

Method

Melt the butter and stir in the sugar. Add the biscuit crumbs and mix well. Lightly grease a 20 cm (8 in) flan ring and press in the crumb mixture, covering the base and sides. Chill the case in the refrigerator while preparing the filling.

Put the raisins and water into a pan and simmer for 10 minutes. Mix the cornflour with 1 additional tablespoon of water. Stir into the raisins and add the spices and brown sugar. Heat gently until the sugar has dissolved and the mixture is thick. Leave to cool for 15 minutes, stirring often. Pour into the crumb case and chill.

Tiffin

Quick to make, these chocolate slices are popular with a drink, or may be used as a sweet course when topped with cream or ice cream.

Makes 15 biscuits
Time Preparation 10 minutes

Ingredients

250 g (8 oz) plain chocolate	50 g (2 oz) chopped walnuts
250 g (8 oz) McVitie's Rich Tea Biscuits	125 g (4 oz) hard margarine, cut into small pieces
2 teaspoons cocoa	1 tablespoon golden syrup
50 g (2 oz) glacé cherries, finely chopped	15 g (½ oz) sugar

Method

Put half the chocolate into a bowl over hot water and leave it until melted. Crush the biscuits into crumbs. Mix the crumbs with the cocoa, cherries and walnuts. Stir the margarine, syrup and sugar into the chocolate until just melted.

Stir the crumbs into the chocolate mixture. Grease a 27.5 cm × 17.5 cm (11 in × 7 in) shallow tin. Press in the crumb mixture. Melt the remaining chocolate in a clean bowl over hot water and spread it on top of the biscuit mixture. Leave until cool and mark into 15 biscuits just before the chocolate sets. Cut and remove from the tin when cold.

Top Tiffin; *Bottom* No-bake Christmas Cake

No-bake Christmas Cake

This colourful fruit cake makes a pleasant alternative to the traditional version.

Makes 1 × 22.5 cm (9 in) cake
Time Preparation 20 minutes (plus chilling time)

Ingredients

250 g (8 oz) marshmallows	125 g (4 oz) chopped walnuts
10 tablespoons evaporated milk	25 g (1 oz) angelica, chopped
3 tablespoons orange juice	½ teaspoon ground cinnamon
350 g (12 oz) mixed sultanas and raisins	½ teaspoon ground nutmeg
250 g (8 oz) stoned dates, chopped	¼ teaspoon ground cloves
250 g (8 oz) mixed candied peel, chopped	750 g (1½ lb) McVitie's Digestive Biscuits, crushed into crumbs
125 g (4 oz) glacé cherries, chopped	icing sugar, for sprinkling

Method

Chop the marshmallows into small pieces with wet scissors. Cover with the milk and orange juice. Stir in the sultanas, raisins, dates, peel, cherries, walnuts, angelica and spices. Add all the ingredients to the crushed biscuits and mix thoroughly. Grease and line a 22.5 cm (9 in) round cake tin. Press in the mixture, cover with foil and chill for 48 hours.

Turn out and sprinkle with a little icing sugar. Store in the refrigerator.

Chocolate Truffle Cakes

These delicious cakes may be made from chocolate cake, fruit cake or sponge cake crumbs, but they look and taste very expensive.

Makes 12 cakes
Time Preparation 15 minutes (plus chilling time)

Ingredients

250 g (8 oz) stale cake	4 rounded tablespoons
25 g (1 oz) cocoa	apricot jam
1 tablespoon rum or brandy	3 tablespoons water
8 tablespoons syrup from	125 g (4 oz) chocolate
canned fruit or diluted	vermicelli
orange squash	icing sugar, for sprinkling

Method

Chop the cake into coarse crumbs in a food processor or blender, or break it up with a fork. Stir in the cocoa until evenly coloured. Add the rum or brandy and syrup or squash to make a soft but firm mixture.

Roll into 12 balls, without pressing the mixture too hard. Chill for 1 hour in the refrigerator.

Put the jam and water into a pan and heat gently until the jam has melted. Stir well. Put the chocolate vermicelli on a plate. Using two spoons, dip the cakes quickly into the jam to coat them lightly, and roll them in the vermicelli. Put the cakes into paper cases, leave for 1 hour, and then sprinkle the tops with icing sugar.

Italian Torrone

This favourite Italian delicacy contains biscuits broken into small pieces. It may be served as a cake or as a sweet course.

Makes 1 × 20 cm (8 in) cake
Time Preparation 15 minutes (plus chilling time)

Ingredients

125 g (4 oz) soft margarine	50 g (2 oz) McVitie's
75 g (3 oz) cocoa	Digestive Biscuits
150 g (5 oz) ground almonds	25 g (1 oz) glacé cherries,
1 egg, beaten	chopped
125 g (4 oz) caster sugar	25 g (1 oz) chopped walnuts
2 tablespoons water	12 walnut halves, to
	decorate

Method

Cream the margarine and cocoa until well mixed. Add the almonds and egg and mix well. Put the sugar and water into a pan and heat gently until the sugar has dissolved. Pour on to the almond mixture and beat well.

Break the biscuits into almond-sized pieces. Stir into the mixture with the cherries and chopped nuts. Grease and base-line a 20 cm (8 in) round tin. Put in the mixture, smooth the top with a knife and chill until firmly set.

Turn on to a plate and decorate with walnuts.

Chocolate Fudge Flan

A biscuit crust is filled with a rich chocolate and nut cream, and may be served with a topping of whipped cream.

Makes 1 × 22.5 cm (9 in) flan
Time Preparation 10 minutes (plus chilling time)

Ingredients

125 g (4 oz) butter	150 g (5 oz) McVitie's
125 g (4 oz) sugar	Digestive Biscuits,
	crushed into crumbs

Filling

250 g (8 oz) butter	½ teaspoon vanilla essence
150 g (5 oz) caster sugar	125 g (4 oz) marshmallows
2 eggs, beaten	125 g (4 oz) chopped walnuts
50 g (2 oz) plain chocolate	

Method

Melt the butter and stir in the sugar. Add the biscuit crumbs and mix well. Lightly butter a 22.5 cm (9 in) flan ring and press in the crumb mixture, covering the base and sides. Put the case into the refrigerator while preparing the filling.

Cream the butter and sugar until light and fluffy. Work in the eggs, a little at a time. Melt the chocolate in a bowl over hot water, and work it into the butter mixture with the vanilla essence. Chop the marshmallows into small pieces with wet scissors. Fold the marshmallow pieces and nuts into the creamed mixture and spoon into the crumb case. Chill until the filling is firm.

No-bake Chocolate Cake

This is excellent as a cake, but is also excellent served as a sweet course.

Makes 1 × 17.5 cm (7 in) cake
Time Preparation 15 minutes (plus chilling time)

Ingredients

125 g (4 oz) apricot jam	175 g (6 oz) sweet biscuits,
75 g (3 oz) butter	crushed into crumbs
25 g (1 oz) cocoa	150 ml (¼ pint) double
50 g (2 oz) dark soft brown	cream
sugar	50 g (2 oz) plain chocolate,
	coarsely grated

Method

Put the jam, butter and cocoa into a pan and heat until the jam and butter have melted and the mixture is smooth. Remove from the heat and stir in the sugar and biscuit crumbs.

Lightly grease and base-line a 17.5 cm (7 in) round tin. Press in the mixture and chill until firm. Turn out of the tin on to a serving plate.

Whip the cream until it forms soft peaks and spoon it over the surface of the cake. Sprinkle the grated chocolate over the cream.

Top Biscuit Cake (p. 36); *Bottom*
Marmalade Cake (p. 30)

Microwave
baking

*I*t is not difficult to prepare cakes and biscuits in the microwave oven, and basic preparation is the same as for conventional ovens. There is, however, a slight adjustment to ingredients, and considerable adjustment in timing.

Appearance of Cakes

Cooks who are used to the appearance of a baked cake from a traditional oven may find it difficult at first to adjust to the slightly different appearance of microwaved cakes. While they rise well in the oven, cakes do not brown or achieve the traditional golden crust; the surface looks just set but still moist. But if a cake is left to stand (in the same way as other microwave dishes) it finishes cooking and achieves a more conventional appearance. It is important to resist the temptation to bake the cake for a few minutes longer to get a conventional appearance, because the end result will be like a rock.

In order to make cakes look rich and appetising, wholemeal flour and brown sugar may be used to give a browner cake – an advantage now that 'healthier' cakes are popular. Chocolate and dried fruit give natural colour to cakes, and some cooks like to add a little gravy browning to enhance the colour of fruit cakes. If a cake is naturally pale, such as a sponge cake, it needs to be finished with icing, or a sprinkling of nuts.

Choosing a Recipe

Some popular cakes cannot be made successfully in a microwave oven, but there is a good range of recipes which work well and which are very appetising. Fatless sponges do not bake well, and neither do scones and rock cakes which should have a crisp exterior. Bread becomes close and unappetising, but the oven is useful for speeding up the rising of doughs (see below). Delicate biscuits are not very successful but those containing wholemeal flour and other textured ingredients work well.

On the plus side, chocolate cakes and fruit cakes are very good, and so are homely cakes containing oats, wholemeal flour, nuts, brown sugars and fresh fruit such as apples or bananas. Tray-bakes with plenty of textured ingredients are particularly successful.

Adapting a Recipe

If a favourite recipe for a conventional cooker is to be adapted for microwaving, a little extra liquid will be needed because cakes dry quickly in the microwave oven. Milk is preferable to water for improving the keeping quality. Self-raising flour may be used, but if using plain flour and baking powder, reduce the raising agent by one-quarter, as cakes rise more easily. Sugar and fat burn very quickly in a microwave oven, so recipes which are very high in either or both are best avoided, as are sugar toppings added before baking.

Leave a cake to stand when it comes out of the microwave oven to finish the cooking process.

Line a round dish with roasting film for flexibility and easy removal of the cake.

Place a container of water in the microwave oven when proving dough to improve the quality of the bread.

Equipment

It is important to check the manufacturer's instructions for the microwave oven before baking, to see if there are any special factors to be considered. A turntable is an advantage for even baking, but otherwise the cake must be turned once or twice during cooking to ensure an even rise.

The correct size of container must be used, but metal tins are not suitable. There are many special containers available, but many kinds of ordinary household dishes are suitable. Ovenglass or china is excellent, if special dishes are not available. Straight-sided soufflé dishes or casseroles are suitable for deep cakes, ceramic flan dishes for shallow ones, and lasagne dishes for tray-bakes. An ovenglass loaf dish can be very useful, and a ring mould is often recommended for cakes as the heat is distributed evenly and quickly. (In a deep plain dish a cake may take a long time to cook and the centre remains soggy.)

Paper cases may be used for individual cakes, or indented muffin dishes are available for small items. A flat plate is useful for biscuit mixtures.

Preparing a Recipe

Mixing methods are the same as for conventional cakes, but the ingredients must be very thoroughly blended so that there are no lumps of sugar or fat which might burn.

Containers should not be greased and floured as this creates an unpleasant film on the surface of the cake. The dish may be lightly greased and base-lined or fully lined with greaseproof paper, as recommended in the recipe. Roasting film is very flexible and useful for lining odd-shaped containers such as ring moulds.

If a mixture is left to stand in a container for up to 10 minutes before baking, air bubbles will begin to form and the cake will be very light. For a deep cake, such as a fruit cake, it is a good idea to stand the container on an upturned plate in the oven as this helps the centre of the cake to cook through. Containers should be only half-full.

When baked, the cake will look slightly soft and sticky, but it will firm up if left to stand in the container for the recommended time before turning out.

Biscuits or small cakes should be arranged in a circle on the outer edge of a plate or dish, with a little space between, to ensure even cooking.

Microwave Tips

Even if a microwave oven is not used for complete baking, it is a useful piece of equipment for the home baker. Chocolate or butter can be melted quickly in a bowl, without messing about with pans of hot water; nuts can be lightly browned; liquid can be heated for yeast doughs without dirtying a pan; and fruit can be plumped by heating in a little water, juice or tea.

Proving Dough

It is easy to speed up the rising of bread dough in a microwave oven. Cover the dough in a bowl with roasting film and microwave on High for 10 seconds. Leave to stand for 10 minutes and microwave for 10 seconds. Repeat the process until the dough is sufficiently risen. If a mug of water is placed in the oven with the dough, this will improve the quality of the bread. The liquid for yeast dough may also be heated in the oven, and so may the mixing bowl and flour.

Time Adjustment

The recipes in this section have been tested with a 600-watt output microwave oven. For a 500-watt oven, *increase* the timing by 25 seconds for each minute. For a 700-watt oven, *decrease* the timing by 25 seconds for each minute. Check the manufacturer's instructions if an oven has variable control and different names for the power settings (the majority of cakes in this section are cooked on High or Full Power). If in doubt, look through the manufacturer's recipes for a similar recipe and adjust the oven accordingly.

Marmalade Cake

This lovely cake with an attractive topping may be varied according to the type of marmalade used: try a medium-cut orange variety, or experiment with lemon or lime marmalade.

Makes 1 × 20 cm (8 in) cake
Time Preparation 10 minutes, Baking 8 minutes, Standing 5 minutes
Power Setting High

Ingredients

200 ml (7 fl oz) vegetable oil	175 g (6 oz) plain wholemeal flour
4 rounded tablespoons marmalade	175 g (6 oz) self-raising flour
175 g (6 oz) caster sugar	½ teaspoon bicarbonate of soda
3 eggs	
4 tablespoons milk	

Topping

2 tablespoons dark marmalade	25 g (1 oz) chopped mixed nuts

Method
Put the oil, marmalade, sugar, eggs and milk into a bowl and beat hard until well mixed. Stir the flours and bicarbonate of soda together until evenly coloured. Add the liquid mixture to the flour and beat well.

Line a 20 cm (8 in) straight-sided dish with roasting film. Put in the mixture and microwave for 8 minutes. Leave to stand for 5 minutes, and turn out on to a rack to cool.

When the cake is cold, prepare the topping. Put the marmalade into a small bowl and microwave for 1 minute. Stir in the nuts and spread over the surface of the cake.

Farmhouse Fruit Cake

This light, fruity cake is good with tea or coffee or for a lunch-box or picnic.

Makes 1 × 17.5 cm (7 in) cake
Time Preparation 5 minutes, Baking 7 minutes, Standing 5 minutes
Power Setting High

Ingredients

250 g (8 oz) self-raising wholemeal flour	175 g (6 oz) mixed dried fruit
½ teaspoon baking powder	2 eggs
125 g (4 oz) hard margarine, cut into pieces	5 tablespoons milk
125 g (4 oz) light soft brown sugar	2 teaspoons grated lemon rind

Method
Put the flour and baking powder into a bowl and stir well to mix evenly. Rub in the margarine until the mixture resembles fine breadcrumbs. Stir in the sugar and fruit until evenly distributed. Beat the eggs and milk together and add to the dry ingredients with the lemon rind.

Grease and base-line a 17.5 cm (7 in) straight-sided dish with greaseproof paper. Put in the mixture and microwave for 7 minutes. Leave to stand for 5 minutes, and turn on to a rack to cool.

Lemon Sponge

A ring mould looks most attractive for a cake, but it also helps to microwave the mixture quickly and evenly.

Makes 1 × 20 cm (8 in) ring cake
Time Preparation 10 minutes, Baking 8 minutes, Standing 10 minutes
Power Setting High

Ingredients

175 g (6 oz) butter	175 g (6 oz) wholemeal self-raising flour
175 g (6 oz) light soft brown sugar	pinch of salt
grated rind and juice of 1 lemon	pinch of ground mixed spice
	3 eggs, beaten

Icing and Decoration

75 g (3 oz) butter or soft margarine	grated rind and juice of ½ lemon
175 g (6 oz) icing sugar	mimosa balls and angelica

Method
Cream the butter and sugar until light and fluffy, and add the grated lemon rind. Sieve the flour, salt and spice. Add the flour and eggs alternately to the creamed mixture, and beat in the lemon juice.

Line a 20 cm (8 in) ring mould with roasting film. Put the mixture into the mould and microwave for 8 minutes. Leave to stand for 10 minutes, then turn on to a wire rack to cool.

Cream the butter or soft margarine and icing sugar, add the lemon rind and juice and beat well. Spread the icing over the cake and decorate with mimosa balls and angelica.

Chocolate Cake

Finish this deliciously light chocolate cake with a simple butter icing or with melted chocolate.

Makes 1 × 17.5 cm (7 in) cake
Time Preparation 5 minutes, Baking 6 minutes
Power Setting High

Ingredients

125 g (4 oz) butter	1 large egg (size 1 or 2)
125 g (4 oz) demerara sugar	5 tablespoons milk
200 g (7 oz) self-raising flour	
25 g (1 oz) drinking chocolate powder	

Icing

125 g (4 oz) icing sugar	1 tablespoon cocoa
50 g (2 oz) butter or soft margarine	a little milk

Method
Line a 17.5 cm (7 in) round dish with roasting film. Cream the butter and sugar until light and fluffy. Sieve the flour and chocolate powder together. Beat the egg and milk lightly together. Add the flour and egg alternately to the creamed mixture, beat well, and put into the dish. Microwave for 6 minutes.

Cool in the dish and turn out on to a serving plate.

Cream the icing sugar and fat, and work in the cocoa and a little milk to make a soft icing. Spread the icing on top of the cake.

Apple Walnut Cake

This is a good family cake with a nice fruity taste, finished with a light lemon icing.

Makes 1 × 20 cm (8 in) round cake
Time Preparation 10 minutes, Baking 8 minutes, Standing 15 minutes
Power Setting High

Ingredients

175 g (6 oz) unsalted butter	2 tablespoons golden syrup
125 g (4 oz) caster sugar	175 g (6 oz) self-raising flour
3 eggs, beaten	50 g (2 oz) chopped walnuts
grated rind and juice of 1 lemon	1 eating apple, peeled, cored and finely chopped

Icing and Decoration

50 g (2 oz) unsalted butter	juice of ½ lemon
2 tablespoons milk	walnut halves, to decorate (optional)
200 g (7 oz) icing sugar	

Method

Cream the butter and sugar until light and fluffy. Add the eggs gradually to the creamed mixture. Mix the lemon rind and juice with the syrup and add to the creamed mixture. Sieve the flour and fold it into the mixture with the walnuts and the chopped apple.

Line a 20 cm (8 in) round dish with roasting film. Spoon in the cake mixture, and microwave for 8 minutes. Leave to stand for 15 minutes and turn on to a wire rack to cool.

To make the icing, put the butter and milk into a bowl and microwave for 30 seconds. Beat in the icing sugar and lemon juice. Spread over the top of the cake. If liked, decorate with halved walnuts.

Carrot Cake

An easy microwave version of this popular classic, this cake may be finished with Cream Cheese Icing (page 122), or with a sprinkling of demerara or icing sugar.

Makes 1 × 25 cm (10 in) ring cake
Time Preparation 15 minutes, Baking 8 minutes, Standing 10 minutes
Power Setting High

Ingredients

250 g (8 oz) plain wholemeal flour	4 eggs
2 teaspoons baking powder	2 teaspoons grated orange rind
1 teaspoon ground mixed spice	250 g (8 oz) carrots, grated
300 ml (½ pint) vegetable oil	125 g (4 oz) walnuts, finely chopped
250 g (8 oz) light soft brown sugar	

Method

Stir together the flour, baking powder and spice in a bowl. Put the oil, sugar, eggs and rind into another bowl and beat well together. Add to the dry ingredients with the carrots and walnuts and beat well.

Line a 25 cm (10 in) ring mould with roasting film. Put in the cake mixture and microwave for 8 minutes. Leave to stand for 10 minutes before turning on to a wire rack to cool.

When cold, sprinkle with demerara or icing sugar, or spread with Cream Cheese Icing (page 122).

32 *Top left* Chocolate Delights (p. 36);
Top Right Lemon Sponge (p. 30);
Bottom left Carrot Cake (p. 31);
Bottom right Banana Teabread
(p. 35)

Cup Cakes

These little cakes are just the thing for an unexpected tea party, and the flavours may be varied.

Makes 12 small cakes
Time Preparation 10 minutes, Baking 2 minutes
Power Setting High

Ingredients

50 g (2 oz) butter or soft margarine
50 g (2 oz) caster sugar
125 g (4 oz) self-raising flour
1 egg
3 tablespoons milk
few drops of vanilla essence

Method

Cream the fat and sugar. Sieve the flour. Beat the egg and milk together with the essence. Add the flour and egg mixture alternately to the creamed mixture, beating well between each addition.

Divide the mixture between 12 paper cases. Arrange six cases in a circle on a flat plate, or place them in a microwave muffin mould. Microwave for 2 minutes, and cool on a wire rack. Repeat with the remaining cakes. Finish, if liked, with Glacé Icing (page 121) and decorate with chopped nuts, cherries or grated chocolate.

Variations

Chocolate: Substitute 15 g (½ oz) cocoa for the same amount of flour.
Coffee: Add 1 teaspoon coffee essence instead of vanilla essence.
Fruit: Add 50 g (2 oz) mixed dried fruit.
Orange or lemon: Substitute orange or lemon essence for the vanilla essence in the above recipe, and add ½ teaspoon of the appropriate fruit rind.

Top Date and Nut Loaf; *Bottom* Cup Cakes

Date and Nut Loaf

This simple teabread is very good sliced and spread with butter.

Makes 1 loaf cake
Time Preparation 10 minutes, Baking 9 minutes, Standing 10 minutes
Power Setting High

Ingredients

175 g (6 oz) dark soft brown sugar
50 g (2 oz) soft margarine
125 g (4 oz) plain flour
125 g (4 oz) plain wholemeal flour
pinch of salt
300 ml (½ pint) milk and water mixed
1 teaspoon bicarbonate of soda
1 egg
125 g (4 oz) stoned dates, chopped
50 g (2 oz) chopped mixed nuts

Method

Cream the sugar and margarine until light and fluffy. Work in the flours and salt. Put the milk and water into a mug, and microwave for 2 minutes. Stir in the soda and beat into the cake mixture. Add the egg and beat well. Stir in the dates and nuts.

Line a 1 kg (2 lb) loaf dish with roasting film. Put in the cake mixture and microwave for 9 minutes. Leave to stand for 10 minutes, and turn on to a wire rack to cool. To serve, cut into slices and spread with butter.

Nutty Fingers

This crisp shortbread with nuts may be cut into small fingers which are very good served with ice cream or other light puddings.

Makes 14–16 fingers
Time Preparation 10 minutes, Baking 5 minutes
Power Setting High

Ingredients

150 g (5 oz) plain flour	125 g (4 oz) butter, cut into
25 g (1 oz) ground rice	pieces
pinch of salt	25 g (1 oz) walnuts, finely
50 g (2 oz) caster sugar	chopped

Method

Stir the flour, rice and salt together in a bowl until evenly mixed. Stir in the sugar and rub in the butter until the mixture is like fine breadcrumbs. Stir in the nuts and form into a dough, kneading lightly.

Roll out the dough on a lightly floured board into a 17.5 cm (7 in) square. Cut into 14–16 fingers. Place the fingers on a flat plate and microwave for 2½ minutes. Turn the plate and microwave for a further 2½ minutes. Put a piece of baking parchment on to a wire rack and carefully lift the biscuits on to the rack to cool.

Semi-sweet Biscuits

These are useful biscuits to have in the tin as they are good with cheese as well as with sweet things, and they are very good with tea and coffee.

Makes 12–14 biscuits
Time Preparation 10 minutes, Baking 3 minutes, Standing 2 minutes
Power Setting High

Ingredients

125 g (4 oz) butter	½ teaspoon baking powder
125 g (4 oz) porridge oats	pinch of salt
50 g (2 oz) plain wholemeal	25 g (1 oz) demerara sugar
flour	a little milk
50 g (2 oz) self-raising flour	

Method

Put the butter into a bowl and microwave for 1 minute to melt it. Mix in the oats, flours, baking powder, salt and sugar and mix to a stiff dough, adding a little milk if necessary.

Roll out the dough on a lightly floured board until it is about 0.75 cm (¼ in) thick. Cut into 5 cm (2 in) rounds with a plain cutter. Line a plate with roasting film and put on 6–8 biscuits at regular intervals. Microwave for 3 minutes. Leave to stand for 2 minutes and lift on to a wire rack to cool. Repeat with the remaining biscuits.

Top Nutty Fingers; *Bottom* Semi-sweet Biscuits

Banana Teabread

The fruit for this teabread is softened and made plump by pre-cooking in tea. It is a moist teabread which is delicious served sliced and buttered.

Makes 1 × 1 kg (2 lb) loaf
Time Preparation 15 minutes, Baking 9 minutes, Standing 5 minutes
Power Setting High

Ingredients

150 g (5 oz) sultanas	125 g (4 oz) light soft brown
150 g (5 oz) chopped dates	sugar
175 ml (6 fl oz) cold tea	1 medium banana, mashed
(without milk)	1 egg, beaten
175 g (6 oz) self-raising flour	pinch of ground ginger

Method

Put the dried fruit and tea into a bowl, cover with roasting film and pierce the film once or twice. Microwave for 8 minutes and leave to cool.

Sieve the flour into a bowl and stir in the sugar until evenly coloured. Add the fruit mixture and mix well. Add the banana, egg and ginger and beat well. Base-line a 1 kg (2 lb) loaf dish with greaseproof paper and grease the sides well. Put in the mixture and microwave for 9 minutes. Leave to stand for 5 minutes before turning out to cool. Serve sliced and buttered.

As soon as Man started to use fire for cooking his food, he must have begun to make bread, although the action of yeast was unknown. Simple mixtures of ground cereals mixed with water were cooked on hot stones as primitive biscuits or soft pancakes, or dough was wrapped around sticks and held over the hot fire to produce a pastry-like bread. This early unleavened bread gave way in the Western world to dough mixed with frothing ale yeast, until compressed baker's yeast made its appearance in the nineteenth century.

Today, results can be predicted accurately if basic instructions are followed carefully (page 15). However perfect the bread, it will be even more acceptable if finished attractively. If a container of water is placed in the oven during baking, the bread will have a crisp crust. Plain loaves painted with rich milk or cream before baking have a gleaming brown crust; beaten eggs give a dark crust, while melted butter or margarine gives a crisp, crunchy crust.

Wholemeal loaves look interesting if brushed with a solution of salt and water before baking, then scattered with cracked wheat (from a health food shop). White bread may be finished with poppy seeds, sesame seeds or crunchy sea salt.

When preparing plain white or wholemeal doughs, it is always using a 1.5 kg (3 lb) quantity of flour. Spare loaves freeze well, or portions of the risen dough may be transformed into secondary baked items such as Calzone, Lardy Cake or Doughnuts.

White Bread

This is a good basic bread for everyday use. It is worth making the full quantity as bread freezes so well.

Makes 4 × 500 g (1 lb) loaves
Time Preparation 15 minutes, Proving 2 hours, Baking 35 minutes
Oven Temperature Gas Mark 8/230°C/450°F

Ingredients

1.5 kg (3 lb) white bread flour	25 g (1 oz) fresh yeast or 3 teaspoons dried yeast
25 g (1 oz) salt	750 ml (1¼ pints) lukewarm water
25 g (1 oz) lard, cut into pieces	

Method

Sieve the flour and salt into a bowl and rub in the lard until the mixture is like fine breadcrumbs. Mix the yeast and water and leave until frothing well. Add to the flour and mix to a firm dough. Knead for 10 minutes until the dough is firm and elastic, but not sticky. Put into a greased bowl, cover, and leave in a warm place to prove for 1 hour.

Divide the dough into four pieces and knead each piece thoroughly. Shape to fit greased 500 g (1 lb) loaf tins. Cover and prove for 1 hour until the dough reaches just to the top of the tins. Bake for 35 minutes. The loaves will shrink slightly from the sides of the tins, be golden-brown, and will sound hollow when tapped on the base. Turn out and cool on a wire rack.

Wholemeal Bread

Wholemeal bread is very popular but it must be well kneaded and given plenty of time to prove to ensure lightness. For a paler, lighter-textured loaf, use a mixture of wholemeal and white flours.

Makes 4 × 500 g (1 lb) loaves
Time Preparation 15 minutes, Proving 2 hours, Baking 40 minutes
Oven temperature Gas Mark 8/230°C/450°F

Ingredients

1.5 kg (3 lb) wholemeal bread flour	25 g (1 oz) lard, cut into pieces
25 g (1 oz) salt	50 g (2 oz) fresh yeast or 6 teaspoons dried yeast
25 g (1 oz) soft brown sugar or clear honey	900 ml (1½ pints) lukewarm water
2 teaspoons malt extract (optional)	

Method

Stir together the flour, salt, sugar and malt extract. Rub in the lard. Mix the yeast with the water and leave until frothing well. Add to the dry ingredients and mix to a soft dough. Knead for 10 minutes, cover, and leave in a warm place to prove for 1 hour.

Knead the dough again and divide into four pieces. Shape into round loaves or to fit greased 500 g (1 lb) loaf tins. Cover and leave to prove for 1 hour. Bake for 40 minutes and cool on a wire rack.

French Flutes

Crisp French bread needs a lot of kneading and this is a good bread to make using the dough hook on an electric mixer.

Makes 4 loaves
Time Preparation 30 minutes, Proving 6¼ hours, Baking 40 minutes
Oven Temperature Gas Mark 8/230°C/450°F

Ingredients

1 kg (2 lb) white bread flour	600 ml (1 pint) water
1 teaspoon sugar	15 g (½ oz) salt
25 g (1 oz) fresh yeast or 3 teaspoons dried yeast	25 g (1 oz) butter, melted and cooled

Method

Sieve half the flour into a bowl and stir in the sugar. Put the yeast into a bowl. Heat half the water to lukewarm and add to the yeast. Leave until frothing well. Add to the flour and mix well. Cover and leave in a warm place to prove for 3 hours. Heat the rest of the water to lukewarm and stir in the salt. Pour over the dough and mix until the crusty skin which has formed disappears. Work in the remaining flour and knead for 15 minutes.

Put the dough into a bowl and slap it down. Keep lifting and slapping it down for 5 minutes. Cover, and leave to prove for 2 hours.

Divide the dough into four pieces and roll into balls. Put on a floured board, cover with a cloth and leave for 15 minutes. Roll and pull each ball into a 'sausage' shape. Place the shapes on a clean cloth at intervals and pull the cloth tightly up the sides and between the loaves so that they cannot expand sideways. Cover and prove for 1 hour.

Place the loaves on two greased baking sheets and slash each loaf diagonally three times with a sharp knife. Bake for 30 minutes and then brush with melted butter. Continue baking for 10 minutes, and cool on a wire rack.

Flowerpot Bread

The shape of these loaves is very attractive, and they are easy to make. Clay containers were used to shape bread before tin utensils were in common use.

Makes 2 loaves
Time Preparation 10 minutes, Proving 1½ hours, Baking 35 minutes
Oven Temperature Gas Mark 8/230°C/450°F

Ingredients

250 g (8 oz) wholemeal bread flour	15 g (½ oz) fresh yeast or 1½ teaspoons dried yeast
175 g (6 oz) white bread flour	300 ml (½ pint) lukewarm water
2 teaspoons salt	1 teaspoon sugar
25 g (1 oz) lard, cut into pieces	

Method

Prepare new clay flowerpots before using them. Take two 12.5 cm (5 in) flowerpots and grease them well with oil or lard. Put them into the oven and leave for 30 minutes. Remove and cool them before using. This treatment will enable the pots to hold the dough safely in the oven without cracking.

Mix the wholemeal and white flours and salt in a bowl until evenly coloured. Rub in the lard. Mix the yeast, water and sugar and leave until frothing well. Add to the dry ingredients and mix to a soft dough. Knead until smooth, cover and leave in a warm place to prove for 1 hour.

Knead the dough again and divide into two pieces. Grease the flowerpots and shape the bread to fit them. Place the pots upright on a baking sheet. Cover and leave in a warm place to prove for 30 minutes. Bake for 35 minutes and turn on to a wire rack to cool.

When the bread is cooked, the pots should be cleaned thoroughly, dried and kept for further use.

40   *Top left* Flowerpot Bread (p. 39);
Top Right French Flutes (p. 39);
Bottom left Oaten Loaf (p. 42);
Bottom right Rye Bread (p. 42)

Rye Bread

Dark, rich-flavoured bread is particularly good with cheese and with smoked fish. The bread has a close texture and is excellent for open sandwiches.

Makes 2 loaves
Time Preparation 15 minutes, Proving 2¼ hours, Baking 50 minutes
Oven Temperature Gas Mark 8/230°C/450°F, *then* Gas Mark 2/150°C/350°F

Ingredients

300 g (10 oz) rye flour	25 g (1 oz) fresh yeast
300 g (10 oz) white bread flour	*or* 3 teaspoons dried yeast
1 teaspoon salt	300 ml (½ pint) lukewarm milk and water
1 teaspoon sugar	1 tablespoon black treacle

Glaze

2 teaspoons cornflour	150 ml (¼ pint) boiling water

Method
Stir together the flours, salt and sugar in a bowl. Mix the yeast with the milk and water and leave until frothing well. Add to the dry ingredients with the treacle to make a firm dough. Knead well, cover and leave in a warm place to prove for 1½ hours.

Knead the dough again and shape into two round loaves. Cover and leave to prove for 45 minutes.

To make the glaze, mix the cornflour with a little cold water and add the boiling water. Brush the dough with the glaze and bake for 30 minutes. Reduce the oven temperature. Brush more glaze on to the bread and bake for 15 minutes. Glaze once more and bake for 5 minutes. Cool on a wire rack.

Oaten Loaf

Oats give plenty of texture and flavour to this bread, and a sprinkling of oats on the surface makes the loaves look very attractive.

Makes 1 loaf
Time Preparation 15 minutes, Proving 1½ hours, Baking 30 minutes
Oven Temperature Gas Mark 6/200°C/400°F

Ingredients

300 g (10 oz) white bread flour	300 ml (½ pint) lukewarm milk and water
175 g (6 oz) porridge oats	2 teaspoons sunflower or corn oil
1 teaspoon salt	milk and oats, for finishing
1 teaspoon sugar	
15 g (½ oz) fresh yeast *or* 1½ teaspoons dried yeast	

Method
Sieve the flour into a bowl. Stir in the oats, salt and sugar until evenly mixed. Mix the yeast and lukewarm liquid and leave until frothing well. Mix into the flour with the oil and mix to a soft dough. Knead the dough well, cover and leave in a warm place to prove for 1 hour.

Knead again and divide the dough into three pieces. Roll the pieces into 'sausage' shapes and plait them together loosely. Put on a greased baking sheet, cover and leave to prove for 30 minutes. Brush the surface with a little milk and sprinkle lightly with oats. Bake for 30 minutes and cool on a wire rack.

Milk Twist

This light-textured plaited loaf may be plain, or finished with a little Glacé Icing (page 121).

Makes 1 plaited loaf
Time Preparation 1½ hours, Baking 25 minutes
Oven Temperature Gas Mark 8/230°C/450°F

Ingredients

250 g (8 oz) white bread flour	8 tablespoons warm milk
pinch of salt	1 large (size 1 or 2) egg, beaten
1 teaspoon caster sugar	25 g (1 oz) melted butter
15 g (½ oz) fresh yeast *or* 1 teaspoon dried yeast	milk, for glazing

Method
Sieve the flour and salt into a warm bowl and stir in the sugar. Sprinkle the yeast on to the milk and leave until foaming strongly – this will take about 20 minutes. Mix into the dry ingredients. Add the egg and the butter. Knead thoroughly, cover with a cloth and leave to rise for about 45 minutes, or until the dough has doubled in size.

Knead the dough again on a lightly floured board and form into a long strip. Divide into three, even pieces and plait them loosely together, tucking the ends underneath.

Grease a baking sheet and place the plaited loaf in the centre. Cover with a cloth and leave to stand in a warm place for 15 minutes. Brush well with milk to glaze. Bake for 25 minutes and then cool on a wire rack.

Variation
Add 25 g (1 oz) sugar to the recipe for a sweeter bread. Mix together a little icing sugar with water or lemon juice and spread over the baked loaf. Decorate with chopped nuts, glacé cherries and angelica.

Cheese Bread

This tasty bread is very good served freshly made with a salad.

Makes 2 × 500 g (1 lb) loaves *or* 15 rolls
Time Preparation 10 minutes, Proving 2 hours (rolls 1 hour 20 minutes), Baking 45 minutes (rolls 20 minutes)
Oven Temperature Gas Mark 5/190°C/375°F

Ingredients

500 g (1 lb) white bread flour	15 g (½ oz) fresh yeast
2 teaspoons salt	*or* 1½ teaspoons dried yeast
1 teaspoon mustard	300 ml (½ pint) lukewarm water
pinch of pepper	
125 g (4 oz) Cheddar cheese, grated	

Topping

25 g (1 oz) Cheddar cheese, grated finely	1 teaspoon celery salt

Method

Sieve the flour, salt, mustard and pepper into a bowl and stir in the cheese. Mix the yeast and water and leave until frothing well.

Add the yeast liquid to the dry ingredients and mix to a firm dough. Cover and leave in a warm place to prove for 1 hour. Grease two 500 g (1 lb) loaf tins. Divide the dough in half and shape to fit the tins. (For rolls, shape the dough into 15 balls and place on a greased baking sheet.) Leave loaves to prove for 1 hour, rolls for 20 minutes.

For the topping, mix the cheese and celery salt together and sprinkle on top of the loaves or rolls. Bake for 45 minutes (rolls 20 minutes). Cool on a wire rack.

Poppy Seed Twists

Rich white bread rolls are tied into an attractive knot and sprinkled thickly with poppy seeds. They are particularly delicious and attractive served with salads or ploughman's lunches.

Makes 15 twists
Time Preparation 15 minutes, Proving 45 minutes, Baking 20 minutes
Oven Temperature Gas Mark 7/220°C/425°F

Ingredients

500 g (1 lb) white bread flour	15 g (½ oz) fresh yeast
1 teaspoon salt	or 1½ teaspoons dried
50 g (2 oz) butter or	yeast
margarine, cut into pieces	300 ml (½ pint) lukewarm
15 g (½ oz) sugar	milk
	1 egg, beaten

Topping
1 egg, beaten   15 g (½ oz) poppy seeds

Method

Sieve the flour and salt into a bowl. Rub in the butter or margarine until the mixture is like fine breadcrumbs. Stir in the sugar. Mix the yeast and milk and leave until frothing well. Add to the dry ingredients with the egg and mix to a soft dough. Knead until smooth, cover and leave in a warm place to prove for 30 minutes.

Knead the dough again and divide into 15 pieces. Shape each piece into a 'sausage' about 15 cm (6 in) long, and tie each piece in a loose knot. Place on a greased baking sheet, cover and leave to prove for 15 minutes.

Brush the surface of each twist with egg and sprinkle with poppy seeds. Bake for 20 minutes. Cool on a wire rack.

Buttery Rowies

An Aberdeen speciality, these rolls have a light, flaky texture and are delicious freshly baked and served warm.

Makes 15 rolls
Time Preparation 20 minutes, Proving 1½ hours, Baking 20 minutes
Oven Temperature Gas Mark 6/200°C/400°F

Right Poppy Seed Twists; *Left* Buttery Rowies

Ingredients

500 g (1 lb) white bread flour	300 ml (½ pint) lukewarm
1 teaspoon salt	water
15 g (½ oz) caster sugar	175 g (6 oz) butter
25 g (1 oz) fresh yeast	75 g (3 oz) lard
or 3 teaspoons dried yeast	

Method

Sieve the flour and salt into a bowl and stir in the sugar. Mix the yeast and water and leave until frothing well. Add the yeast mixture to the dry ingredients and work to a soft dough. Knead the dough for 10 minutes, cover, and leave in a warm place to prove for 1 hour.

Knead the dough again and roll out into a rectangle on a lightly floured surface. Mix the butter and lard until well blended together and divide into three portions. Dot one portion of fat all over the dough. Fold down the top third of the dough and fold the bottom third over it. Press the edges with a rolling pin to seal them. Give the dough a half-turn and roll out again. Repeat the process with the other two portions of fat, and roll out lightly. Divide into 15 pieces and form each one into an oval shape.

Grease and flour two baking sheets. Put on the rolls, cover and leave in a warm place to prove for 30 minutes. Bake for 20 minutes and serve warm.

Pumpernickel

This is a very dark, close-textured bread which is good with salt meats, fish and cheese. Cut in thin slices and well buttered, pumpernickel makes a good base for open sandwiches or cocktail canapés.

Makes 1 loaf
Time Preparation 10 minutes, Cooking 3 hours

Ingredients
500 g (1 lb) rye flour
1 teaspoon salt
300 ml (½ pint) lukewarm
  water

2 tablespoons black treacle

Method
Grease a 600 ml (1 pint) pudding basin or a stone jam jar. Stir the flour and salt together and add the water and treacle. Mix very well to a soft dough.

Put the mixture into the container, and cover with greaseproof paper and foil, and tie securely with string. Put into a pan of boiling water so that the water comes half-way up the container. Cover with a lid and simmer for 3 hours, topping up the water occasionally.

Turn the bread out and cool on a wire rack. When cold, wrap in greaseproof paper and foil and store in the refrigerator. Serve cut in very thin slices with unsalted butter.

Top Challah (p. 45); *Bottom* Pumpernickel

Swedish Limpa

This is a rich, dark bread with a flavouring of caraway seeds. Dried yeast does not work well in this mixture, so only fresh yeast should be used.

Makes 1 loaf
Time Preparation 15 minutes, Proving 4¾ hours, Baking 45 minutes
Oven Temperature Gas Mark 5/190°C/375°F

Ingredients
200 ml (7 fl oz) brown ale
125 g (4 oz) black treacle
1 tablespoon vinegar
25 g (1 oz) caraway seeds
15 g (½ oz) fresh yeast
25 g (1 oz) lard, cut into
  small pieces

250 g (8 oz) white bread
  flour
250 g (8 oz) rye flour
1 teaspoon salt

Method
Put the ale, treacle, vinegar and caraway seeds into a pan and heat gently until lukewarm. Remove from the heat and add the crumbled yeast. Stir until dissolved, and then stir in the pieces of lard.

Put the flour and salt into a warm bowl and pour on the warm liquid. Beat hard to form a firm dough. Knead for 5 minutes until smooth. Put the dough into an oiled bowl, cover with a cloth, and leave in a warm place for about 3 hours, until doubled in size. Knead again, cover, and leave to rise for 45 minutes.

Knead the dough for 5 minutes and shape into a round loaf. Put on to a greased baking sheet and cover with a cloth. Leave to rise for 1 hour, until doubled in size, then bake for 45 minutes. Cool on a wire rack.

Pitta Pockets

Pitta bread is a flat bread, oval in shape, which forms a pocket during baking. It is the ideal bread for snacks and picnics, as a filling of salad with meat, fish, eggs or cheese can be safely contained in it.

Makes 6 pitta pockets
Time Preparation 15 minutes, Baking 10 minutes
Oven Temperature Gas Mark 7/190°C/425°F

Ingredients
750 g (1½ lb) white or wholemeal dough, risen (pp. 38–9)

Method
Knead the dough and divide it into six equal pieces. Form the pieces into balls with the hands and roll out each piece into a 20 cm (8 in) circle. Fold each circle in half and press the edges together firmly. Shape into ovals and place on a floured surface. Lightly flour the tops and cover with a cloth.

Put two baking sheets into the oven and leave for about 10 minutes until very hot. Take the baking sheets out of the oven and put on the pieces of dough. Bake for 10 minutes.

Lift the pitta pockets off the baking sheets and wrap them in a clean cloth to keep them soft.

Top Grissini; *Bottom* Calzone

Grissini

These Italian bread sticks, usually served from a tall container, are delicious eaten with unsalted butter.

Makes 30 bread sticks
Time Preparation 25 minutes, Proving 35 minutes, Baking 30 minutes
Oven Temperature Gas Mark 4/180°C/350°F

Ingredients

15 g (½ oz) fresh yeast *or* 1½ teaspoons dried yeast	500 g (1 lb) white or wholemeal bread flour
½ teaspoon caster sugar	25 g (1 oz) butter or hard margarine, melted
300 ml (½ pint) lukewarm milk	1 teaspoon salt milk, for glazing

Method

Stir the yeast and sugar into the lukewarm milk. Put 125 g (4 oz) flour into a bowl and add the yeast liquid, stirring well until thoroughly mixed. Leave for 15 minutes in a warm place until frothy.

Work in the melted fat and then the remaining flour and salt. Work together to form a fairly stiff dough. Cover, and leave to stand for 15 minutes.

Knead the dough on a lightly floured board, and divide into 30 equal pieces. Roll each piece with the hands to form a stick about 25 cm (10 in) long. Place the sticks on two greased baking sheets, and leave in a warm place for 20 minutes. Brush with milk and bake for 30 minutes.

Lift the sticks off carefully and cool on a wire rack.

Calzone

This popular Italian snack is easier to eat in the hand than pizza, and it is most delicious served warm.

Makes 8 pieces
Time Preparation 15 minutes, Proving 15 minutes, Baking 20 minutes
Oven Temperature Gas Mark 7/220°C/425°F

Ingredients
750 g (1½ lb) white bread dough, risen (p. 38)

Filling

250 g (8 oz) cooked ham, sliced thinly	4 teaspoons olive oil salt and pepper
250 g (8 oz) Bel Paese cheese, sliced	

Method

Knead the dough and divide it into eight equal pieces. Form each piece into a ball with the hands and roll each ball into a 15 cm (6 in) circle.

Fold each piece of ham to fit half of each circle and top with a piece of cheese. Sprinkle with olive oil, and season well with salt and pepper. Fold over the top of each circle to form a turnover, and press the edges together to seal them.

Put the turnovers on to a greased baking sheet, cover, and leave to stand for 15 minutes, until lightly risen. Bake for 20 minutes.

Variation

For extra flavour, add 1 large sliced tomato to each circle and sprinkle with Parmesan cheese. A few stoned black olives may be added if liked. Proceed as described in the recipe above.

Chapati

A chapati is unleavened bread like a pancake, eaten hot with curry, and cooked on a griddle or heavy frying pan.

Makes 6 chapatis
Time Preparation 20 minutes, Proving 3 hours

Ingredients
250 g (8 oz) wholemeal flour   butter, for cooking
8 tablespoons water

Method
Put the flour into a bowl and work in the water to make a stiff dough. Knead well, so that the dough is pliable. Put the dough into a lightly oiled bowl, cover with a cloth, and leave to stand for 3 hours.

Knead the dough again and cut into six equal-sized pieces. Shape each piece into a ball, then flatten on a lightly floured board and roll out so that each circle measures about 15 cm (6 in) in diameter.

Grease a griddle or heavy frying pan, and when it is hot, put on a chapati. Cook for 15 seconds and turn over, cooking until brown spots appear on the underside. Turn again and press gently round the edges with a palette knife until the chapati starts to rise in the centre. Lift off the griddle and wrap in a clean cloth to keep soft and hot until all the circles have been cooked. Serve at once, if liked, spread with butter on one side.

Nan

There are many varieties of nan in India, often cooked in a Tandoori oven which gives a smoky flavour. This version comes from the Punjab and is particularly good with kebabs and other grills.

Makes 4 individual breads
Time Preparation 20 minutes, Proving 30 minutes, Baking 7 minutes
Oven Temperature Gas Mark 8/230°C/450°F

Ingredients
5 tablespoons milk
5 tablespoons natural
  yoghurt
1 teaspoon caster sugar
25 g (1 oz) fresh yeast
  or 3 teaspoons dried yeast
300 g (10 oz) white bread
  flour
½ teaspoon bicarbonate of
  soda
¼ teaspoon salt
1 egg, beaten
melted butter, for glazing
milk, for glazing
4 teaspoons sesame seeds

Method
Put the milk and yoghurt into a pan and stir to mix them well. Heat gently until lukewarm. Take off the heat and stir in the sugar and yeast. Leave to stand until the mixture is frothing strongly. Sieve the flour, soda and salt into a bowl and make a well in the centre. Add the yeast liquid and egg and work together to form a soft, smooth dough.

Knead the dough on a lightly floured board until very springy. Put it into a lightly oiled bowl, cover, and leave to prove for about 30 minutes, until not quite doubled in size.

Divide the dough into four equal pieces and form into balls with the hands. Roll the balls into flat, oval pancakes about 25 cm (10 in) long. Cover the top rack of the oven with a piece of foil. Brush the top of each pancake with melted butter. Turn them over, brush with milk and sprinkle with sesame seeds. Place on top of the foil and bake for 7 minutes. Serve hot and freshly baked.

Top Chapati; *Bottom* Nan

Top Bath Buns (p. 50); *Bottom* Selkirk Bannock (p. 51)

*T*eabreads and buns

*T*he earliest forms of cake were in fact cake-breads, nothing more than basic bread dough with a little extra fat, sweetening, dried fruit and spice, baked in the cooling oven when the main bread had been finished, and served as a treat for a meal at the end of a working day. Sometimes, the extra ingredients were worked into the dough; sometimes, they were layered with plain dough. These breads and buns were varied and made to look particularly attractive by being brushed with a little milk or water and sugar immediately after baking to provide a sweet, sticky surface.

When yeast was not available, savoury and sweet teabreads were concocted with self-raising flour, or plain flour and a raising agent, to give a result half-way between bread and cake. These teabreads are now popular to serve sliced with or without butter, and they are much liked by people who do not care for cakes.

Bath Buns

Bath was a fashionable spa and there were many good bakers to cater for visitors. The Bath Bun dates from Georgian times and is distinguished by the flavouring of sultanas, candied peel and lemon, and by the topping of crushed sugar.

Makes 12–18 buns
Time Preparation 20 minutes, Proving 1 hour, Baking 15 minutes
Oven Temperature Gas Mark 8/230°C/450°F

Ingredients

350 g (12 oz) white bread flour	2 eggs, beaten
pinch of salt	75 g (3 oz) sugar
125 g (4 oz) butter, cut into pieces	75 g (3 oz) sultanas
15 g (½ oz) fresh yeast or 1½ teaspoons dried yeast	25 g (1 oz) mixed candied peel, chopped
	grated rind of 1 lemon
	beaten egg, to glaze
65 ml (2½ fl oz) lukewarm milk	cube sugar, lightly crushed

Method

Sieve the flour and salt into a warm bowl. Rub in the butter until the mixture is like fine breadcrumbs. Sprinkle the yeast into the lukewarm milk, and leave until frothing well. Add the yeast liquid to the flour with the eggs, and mix to a soft dough. Cover, and leave in a warm place for 45 minutes.

Knead in the sugar, sultanas, peel and lemon rind. Form into 12–18 rough balls. Put the balls on to two greased baking sheets and flatten them slightly with a hand. Leave in a warm place for 15 minutes. Brush with beaten egg and sprinkle with crushed sugar cubes. Bake for 15 minutes, and cool on a wire rack.

Selkirk Bannock

A bannock is a large flat loaf of cake-bread which was originally baked on a griddle. The richer versions were often used as celebration cakes in Scotland.

Makes 3 bannocks
Time Preparation 20 minutes, Proving 1½ hours, Baking 25 minutes
Oven Temperature Gas Mark 7/220°C/425°F

Ingredients

500 g (1 lb) sultanas	1 teaspoon salt
300 ml (½ pint) milk	75 g (3 oz) butter, cut into
25 g (1 oz) fresh yeast	pieces
or 3 teaspoons dried yeast	75 g (3 oz) sugar
500 g (1 lb) white bread flour	beaten egg, for glazing

Method

Put the sultanas into a bowl, just cover them with boiling water, and leave to stand for 20 minutes. While the sultanas are soaking, heat the milk to lukewarm. Remove from the heat and sprinkle in the yeast. Leave the mixture until frothing well. Drain the sultanas well, and then dry them on kitchen paper.

Sieve the flour and salt together. Rub in the butter until the mixture is like fine breadcrumbs. Stir in the sugar until evenly mixed. Add the yeast liquid and mix to a soft dough. Add the sultanas and work them in gently, as they will be rather soft. Cover the dough, and leave in a warm place for 45 minutes.

Divide the dough into three pieces and shape into balls with the hands. Place on two greased baking sheets and flatten slightly with the hand. Cover, and leave in a warm place for 45 minutes. Brush lightly with beaten egg, and bake for 25 minutes. Cool on a wire rack.

Cheese and Nut Bread

For those who prefer a savoury teabread, this loaf is flavoured with cheese, nuts and herbs.

Makes 1 loaf
Time Preparation 10 minutes, Baking 1 hour
Oven Temperature Gas Mark 4/180°C/350°F

Ingredients

125 g (4 oz) plain wholemeal flour	pepper
125 g (4 oz) self-raising flour	75 g (3 oz) hard margarine
2 teaspoons baking powder	125 g (4 oz) Cheddar cheese, grated
1 teaspoon mustard powder	50 g (2 oz) chopped walnuts
1 teaspoon salt	2 eggs, beaten
1 teaspoon dried mixed herbs	150 milk (¼ pint) milk

Method

Stir together the flours, baking powder, mustard, salt, herbs and pepper. Rub in the margarine until the mixture is like fine breadcrumbs. Stir in the cheese and walnuts until well mixed. Add the egg and milk and beat well.

Grease and base-line a 500 g (1 lb) loaf tin. Put in the mixture and bake for 1 hour. Cool in the tin for 10 minutes and then on a wire rack. Serve sliced and buttered.

Top Lardy Cake; *Bottom* Cheese and Nut Bread

51

Lardy Cake

Like so many early sweet breads, this was originally made from part of a batch of bread dough, but it is easy to make freshly. The fat, sugar and fruit make a rich mixture, and the cake is good either fresh, or sliced, toasted and buttered.

Makes 1 × 17.5 cm (7 in) square cake
Time Preparation 20 minutes, Proving 1¾ hours, Baking 30 minutes
Oven Temperature Gas Mark 8/230°C/450°F

Ingredients

250 g (8 oz) white bread flour	150 ml (¼ pint) lukewarm milk
¼ teaspoon ground mixed spice	50 g (2 oz) lard
¼ teaspoon salt	50 g (2 oz) sugar
7 g (¼ oz) fresh yeast	175 g (6 oz) mixed dried fruit
or 1 teaspoon dried yeast	2 teaspoons sugar, for glazing

Method

Sieve the flour, spice and salt into a bowl. Sprinkle the yeast on to the lukewarm milk and leave until frothing well. Add the yeast liquid to the flour, and work to a soft dough. Knead well, cover, and leave in a warm place for 45 minutes.

Roll out the dough to form a rectangle, about 0.75 cm (¼ in) thick. Spread with half the lard, and sprinkle with half the sugar and half the fruit.

Fold the dough in three, turn it to the left and roll out again. Put on the remaining lard, sugar and fruit. Fold in three, then shape to fit into a greased 17.5 cm (7 in) square tin. Cover, and leave in a warm place for 1 hour.

Mark diamonds on the top of the cake with a knife. Dissolve 2 tablespoons sugar in 1 tablespoon hot water, and brush over the top of the cake. Bake for 30 minutes. Leave in the tin for 10 minutes, and then turn out on to a wire rack to cool with the top upwards. Spoon any syrup which has formed in the base of the tin over the cake.

52 *Top left* Panettone (p. 54); *Top right* Chelsea Buns (p. 56); *Bottom left* Saffron Bread (p. 54); *Bottom right* West Country Cream Splits (p. 56)

60 *Top left* Greek Doughnuts in
Honey Syrup (p. 63); *Top right*
Kugelhopf (p. 62); *Bottom left*
Danish Pastries (p. 64); *Bottom
right* Derbyshire Pikelets (p. 59)

Ad
yeast b
(9 in) ri
in a wa
    Ba
minute
    Wl
dissolv
the boi
and sti
    Pr
cake o
syrup
plate o
    He
Remov
aprico
strawb
into th
the cal

Gr
in

These
and ar

Make
Time
4 min

Ingre
500 g
½ tea
grated
25 g (
    or 3

Hone
250 g
125 g

35 g (

Meth
Sieve
rind.
froth
beat
warr

table
and g

lemo
disso
on a
Spri

*T*he two basic types of pastry are *shortcrust*, made by rubbing fat into flour, and *flaky*, made by layering fat and dough to produce crisp layers. There are a number of variations of these two types which may be used according to taste. For instance, a sweet shortcrust pastry is used for sweet dishes, but wholemeal pastry might be preferred. A cheese pastry is excellent for savoury pies but may be overpowering for some tastes, in which case plain shortcrust or wholemeal pastry may be substituted.

For hints on pastry making and baking, see page 18. When preparing these pastry recipes, remember that 250 g (8 oz) flour will produce about 350 g (12 oz) shortcrust pastry for a finished dish. As a simple guide, just add the weights of flour, fat and such additions as cheese to arrive at the total weight of pastry. Any surplus pastry may be used to make small tarts or savouries, or to decorate pies. It is not possible to give the exact amount of pastry needed to line or cover a container, as this will depend whether the dough is rolled thinly or thickly, but the amount given in each recipe is a pretty accurate guide. If you are using the pastry from these recipes for a dish not given in the book, the suggested oven temperatures are the ideal ones for this type of pastry, but they may be varied slightly according to the filling used.

Shortcrust Pastry

This is the basic pastry which may be used for either savoury or sweet dishes.

Makes 350 g (12 oz) pastry
Time Preparation 10 minutes, Baking 20–25 minutes
Oven Temperature Gas Mark 7/220°C/425°F

Ingredients

250 g (8 oz) plain flour
½ teaspoon salt
50 g (2 oz) hard margarine, cut into pieces

50 g (2 oz) lard, cut into pieces
2–3 tablespoons iced water

Method

Sieve together the flour and salt. Rub in the fat until the mixture is like fine breadcrumbs. Add the water and mix to a stiff dough. Turn on to a lightly floured board and knead very lightly until just smooth. Roll out to the required shape and thickness, and bake for 20–25 minutes.

Wholemeal Shortcrust Pastry

This version of wholemeal pastry made with egg yolks gives a lovely crumbly texture. The pastry is a little fragile, but if it is rolled out on a piece of foil, it can easily be lifted into place.

Makes 400 g (14 oz) pastry
Time Preparation 10 minutes, Baking 20–25 minutes
Oven Temperature Gas Mark 7/220°C/425°F

Ingredients

250 g (8 oz) wholemeal plain flour	2 egg yolks
½ teaspoon salt	1 tablespoon iced water
100 g (4 oz) block vegetable margarine, cut into pieces	

Method
Stir the flour and salt together in a bowl. Rub in the margarine until the mixture looks like fine breadcrumbs. Beat the egg yolks and water together and work into the dry ingredients to make a firm dough. Form the dough into a ball and place on a lightly floured piece of foil. Roll out carefully. If the pastry breaks when placed in a tin, it may be 'patched' with small pieces of pastry which have been cut off. Bake for 20–25 minutes.

Sweet Shortcrust Pastry

A sweet, slightly crumbly pastry, this is delicious for fruit flans and for tartlets. It is a little fragile to handle but is well worth any extra effort.

Makes 300 g (10 oz) pastry
Time Preparation 10 minutes, Baking 20–25 minutes
Oven Temperature Gas Mark 6/200°C/400°F

Ingredients

175 g (6 oz) plain flour	25 g (1 oz) caster sugar
¼ teaspoon salt	1 egg yolk
75 g (3 oz) unsalted butter, cut into pieces	1 tablespoon iced water

Method
Sieve together the flour and salt. Rub in the butter until the mixture is like fine breadcrumbs, and then stir in the sugar. Blend the egg yolk and water together, add to the dry ingredients, and mix to a firm dough. Knead the dough lightly on a floured board, and then roll thinly. Bake for 20–25 minutes.

Flaky Pastry

This is a quickly made, light pastry with an airy flakiness. Although the actual preparation is quick and simple, time must be allowed for chilling the pastry for it to be successful.

Makes 1 kg (2 lb) pastry
Time Preparation 15 minutes, Resting 40 minutes, Baking 20–25 minutes
Oven Temperature Gas Mark 7–8/220–230°C/425–450°F

Ingredients

500 g (1 lb) plain flour	2 teaspoons lemon juice
pinch of salt	300 ml (½ pint) less 1 tablespoon iced water
350 g (12 oz) hard margarine	

Method
Sieve together the flour and salt. Divide the fat into quarters and rub one-quarter, cut into pieces, into the flour. Mix to a pliable dough with lemon juice and water.

Roll out the dough into a 30 cm × 15 cm (12 in × 6 in) rectangle with straight edges. Cut one portion of the remaining fat into small pieces and place these in lines over the top two-thirds of the pastry, leaving a narrow margin round the edges. Fold the bottom third of the pastry upwards and the top third downwards to cover.

Turn the dough so that folded edge is on the left-hand side. Press the edges together with a rolling pin to seal them. Roll the pastry into a rectangle, dot with small pieces of a further portion of fat, and then fold, turn and seal the edges of the pastry as before. Cover, and leave to rest for 20 minutes in a cool place. Repeat the process, but do not rest the dough this time. Repeat the rolling and folding again without fat, and then rest the pastry for 20 minutes.

Finally, roll the pastry out to the required thickness, and bake as specified in the individual recipe.

Flaky Wholemeal Pastry
Prepare in the same way as described in the above recipe, but using plain wholemeal flour and 3 teaspoons baking powder, and a mixture of hard vegetable margarine and lard.

Dot two-thirds of the pastry with butter.

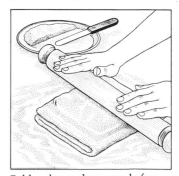

Fold and turn the pastry before sealing the edges with a rolling pin.

Cheese Pastry

The cheese for this pastry must be dry and finely grated; soft, sticky cheese or coarsely grated cheese will not mix in evenly and will make the pastry difficult to handle. For a good flavour, use a little Parmesan cheese with a mature Cheddar.

Makes 500 g (1 lb) pastry
Time Preparation 10 minutes, Baking 25 minutes
Oven Temperature Gas Mark 6/200°C/400°F

Ingredients

250 g (8 oz) plain flour
½ teaspoon salt
pinch of cayenne pepper
125 g (4 oz) hard margarine
  or butter, cut into pieces

125 g (4 oz) hard cheese,
  grated finely
1 egg yolk
2 teaspoons iced water

Method
Sieve together the flour, salt and cayenne pepper. Rub in the fat until the mixture is like fine breadcrumbs. Stir in the cheese until the mixture is evenly coloured. Mix the egg yolk and water, and add to the dry ingredients to make a firm dough. Knead very gently on a lightly floured board until smooth. Roll out as required, and bake for 25 minutes.

Puff Pastry

This is the richest of all pastries. It takes a little care in preparation, and plenty of time is needed for resting the dough.

Makes 1.2 kg (2¼ lb) pastry
Time Preparation 20 minutes, Resting 55 minutes, Baking 25 minutes
Oven Temperature Gas Mark 8/230°C/450°F

Ingredients

500 g (1 lb) plain flour
1 teaspoon salt
500 g (1 lb) butter or hard
  margarine

2 teaspoons lemon juice
300 ml (½ pint) less 1
  tablespoon iced water

Method
Sieve together the flour and salt. Divide the fat into four pieces and rub one-quarter, cut into smaller pieces, into the flour, and make a pliable dough with lemon juice and water. Turn on to a floured board, and knead well until smooth. Leave to rest for 15 minutes in a cool place.

Using two knives, form the remaining fat into a 12.5 cm (5 in) square slab on a floured board. Roll the pastry into a 30 cm × 15 cm (12 in × 6 in) rectangle. Put the block of fat on the top end, leaving a margin of about 1.25 cm (½ in) along the sides and top. Fold over the rest of the dough, press the edges together, and brush off any surplus flour.

Turn the pastry so that the folded edge is on the left-hand side. With the rolling pin, press the open edges together to seal them. Press the rolling pin across the pastry about five times to flatten it. Roll the pastry out into a 30 cm × 15 cm (12 in × 6 in) rectangle, then fold it in three, turn the folded edge to the left, seal the edges, and roll out as before. Fold, turn, and seal the edges. Cover, and leave to rest in a cool place for 20 minutes.

Place the block of fat at the top end of the pastry.

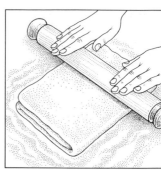

Fold and turn the pastry and press the open edges together using a rolling pin.

Repeat the folding and rolling four more times and rest the pastry for 20 minutes. Roll out as required, and bake for 25 minutes.

Rough Puff Pastry

This quick version of the flaky type of pastry is very good for meat or fish pies or for sausage rolls.

Makes 500 g (1 lb) pastry
Time Preparation 10 minutes, Baking 25 minutes
Oven Temperature Gas Mark 7/220°C/425°F

Ingredients

250 g (8 oz) plain flour
½ teaspoon salt
75 g (3 oz) hard margarine,
  cut into cubes of about
  0.75 cm (¼ in)

75 g (3 oz) lard, cut into
  cubes of about 0.75 cm
  (¼ in)
7 tablespoons iced water

Method
Sieve the flour and salt into a bowl. Add the cubes of fat to the flour, and mix lightly to a soft dough with water.

Roll the dough out on a lightly floured board to a 30 cm × 15 cm (12 in × 6 in) rectangle. Fold the bottom third upwards and the top third downwards. Turn the dough so that the folded edge is on the left-hand side, and seal the edges by pressing them down with the rolling pin. Roll, fold and seal the edges twice more, always keeping the folded edge to the left. If the pastry becomes too soft, chill it between rollings. Roll the pastry out to the required size, and bake for 25 minutes.

Spiced Bacon and Egg Flans

These flans make a pleasant change from the traditional quiche, and they are good hot or cold.

Makes 6 flans
Time Preparation 20 minutes, Baking 40 minutes
Oven Temperature Gas Mark 6/200°C/400°F, *then* Gas Mark 3/160°C/325°F

Ingredients
350 g (12 oz) made cheese pastry (p. 68)

Filling
6 rashers lean bacon, rind removed
150 ml (¼ pint) single cream
2 eggs *plus* 2 egg yolks
¼ teaspoon Tabasco sauce
pinch of mustard powder

Method
Roll out the pastry and line six individual flan tins. Prick the pastry cases well with a fork, and bake blind at the higher oven temperature for 10 minutes.

Chop the bacon rashers finely. Divide the bacon between the pastry cases. Beat together the cream, eggs, egg yolks, Tabasco sauce and mustard powder, and pour the mixture over the bacon. Bake at the lower oven temperature for 30 minutes.

Smoked Haddock Vol-au-vents

A tasty mixture of smoked fish and cheese makes an unusual filling for vol-au-vents, which may be served with vegetables or salad. The filling may also be used for small cocktail vol-au-vents.

Makes 6 vol-au-vents
Time Preparation 20 minutes, Baking 22–25 minutes
Oven Temperature Gas Mark 7/220°C/425°F, *then* Gas Mark 4/180°C/350°F

Ingredients
250 g (8 oz) made puff pastry (p. 68)

Filling
15 g (½ oz) butter
15 g (½ oz) plain flour
150 ml (¼ pint) milk
125 g (4 oz) cooked smoked haddock
125 g (4 oz) Cheddar cheese, grated
1 tablespoon chopped fresh parsley
salt and pepper

Method
Roll out the pastry and cut out six 7.5 cm (3 in) rounds. Mark a 3.75 cm (1½ in) circle in the centre of each round. Rinse a baking sheet in cold water but do not dry it. Place the rounds of pastry on the baking sheet, and bake for 12–15 minutes at the higher oven temperature until well-risen and golden.

While the pastry is cooking, prepare the filling. Melt the butter in a saucepan and work in the flour. Cook for 1 minute over a low heat, stirring well. Take off the heat

Top Smoked Haddock Vol-au-Vents; *Bottom* Spiced Bacon and Egg Flan

and gradually stir in the milk. Return to the heat and bring the sauce to the boil, stirring well. Add the fish, cheese, parsley, salt and pepper, and heat gently.

Remove the lids from the cooked vol-au-vents and scoop out the centres. Divide the fish mixture between them, and replace the lids lightly. Heat at the lower oven temperature for 10 minutes before serving hot.

Buffet Horns

These pastry horns may be filled with chicken, ham or canned salmon. They are easy to serve, and look and taste very good with a selection of salads.

Makes 10 horns
Time Preparation 20 minutes, Baking 15 minutes
Oven Temperature Gas Mark 6/200°C/400°F

Ingredients
500 g (1 lb) made shortcrust pastry (p. 66)
beaten egg, for glazing

Filling
250 g (8 oz) cooked chicken and/or ham, chopped, *or* 250 g (8 oz) canned salmon, well drained
2 tablespoons finely chopped onion
2 tablespoons mayonnaise
½ teaspoon French mustard
salt and pepper

parsley sprigs, for garnishing

Method
Roll out the pastry thinly and cut into 10 thin strips about 20 cm × 2 cm (8 in × ¾ in) long. Wind each strip around a lightly greased cream horn mould, brush with beaten egg and place on a baking sheets. Bake for 15 minutes until golden-brown. Gently twist the baked pastry shapes to remove them from the moulds, and leave them to cool on a wire rack.

Mix the chicken and/or ham, or salmon, with the onion, mayonnaise, mustard, salt and pepper. Just before serving, fill the pastry cases and garnish them with sprigs of parsley.

70   *Top right* Crab Puffs (p. 72);
     Bottom left Buffet Horns (p. 69);
     Bottom centre Special Sausage
     Rolls (p. 72); *Bottom right*
     Cornish Pasties (p. 72)

Cornish Pasties

These traditional pies are very easy to eat at picnics, but they taste just as good served more formally.

Makes 12 pasties
Time Preparation 20 minutes, Baking 50 minutes
Oven Temperature Gas Mark 6/200°C/400°F, *then* Gas Mark 4/180°C/350°F

Ingredients
500 g (1 lb) made shortcrust pastry (p. 66)

Filling

1 small onion	250 g (8 oz) chuck steak, cut
1 small turnip	into very small pieces
1 small carrot	salt and pepper
1 medium potato	

beaten egg, for glazing

Method
Roll out the pastry thinly. Using a small saucepan lid or plate as a guide, cut out twelve × 12.5 cm (5 in) pastry circles.

Peel the vegetables and cut them into small dice. Mix with the meat, and season well with salt and pepper. Divide the filling between the pastry circles. Dampen the edges of each pasty and draw together to form a join across the top. Press the join well together and flute with the fingers.

Place the pasties on a lightly greased baking sheet, and glaze with beaten egg. Bake for 15 minutes at the higher oven temperature. Reduce the heat, and continue baking for 35 minutes. Serve hot or cold.

Crab Puffs

The crab meat used for these puffs may be fresh, canned or frozen. Drain canned fish well, and thaw frozen fish, before flaking it for use.

Makes 24 puffs
Time Preparation 20 minutes, Baking 10 minutes
Oven Temperature Gas Mark 6/200°C/400°F

Ingredients
500 g (1 lb) made shortcrust pastry (p. 66)

Filling

40 g (1½ oz) butter	250 g (8 oz) crab meat,
25 g (1 oz) plain flour	flaked
200 ml (7 fl oz) single cream	salt and pepper
50 g (2 oz) grated Parmesan	1 egg yolk
cheese	1½ tablespoons dry sherry

Method
Roll out the pastry, cut out 24 circles of pastry and line 24 tart tins. Prick the pastry cases well with a fork, and bake blind for 10 minutes. Cool on a wire rack.

Melt the butter in a saucepan and stir in the flour. Cook gently for 1 minute, then gradually add the cream. Stir over a low heat until the sauce thickens. Remove from the heat and stir in 40 g (1½ oz) cheese. Stir until smooth, and then add the crab meat, salt and pepper. Beat the egg yolk and sherry together, and stir into the crab mixture. Spoon into pastry cases and sprinkle with the remaining cheese. Put under a hot grill until golden-brown and puffy. Serve hot.

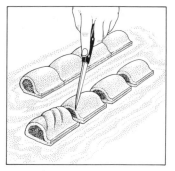

Place the prepared sausages along the centre of the pastry and seal the edges.

Cut and mark each strip.

Special Sausage Rolls

These sausage rolls have the extra flavour of bacon and chutney, and they are delicious with a salad, or served as a snack with drinks.

Makes 8 large sausage rolls
Time Preparation 15 minutes, Baking 25 minutes
Oven Temperature Gas Mark 7/220°C/425°F

Ingredients
500 g (1 lb) made puff pastry (p. 68)

Filling

8 large pork sausages,	2 tablespoons mango
skinned	chutney
8 rashers streaky bacon, rind	
removed	

beaten egg, for glazing

Method
Divide the pastry into two pieces and roll out each piece into a rectangle 40 cm × 12.5 cm (16 in × 5 in). Reshape the skinned sausages neatly with floured hands. Stretch the bacon rashers with the blade of a knife until each one is thin. Spread each rasher with chutney and wrap it round a sausage to cover its full length.

Place four sausages on each strip of pastry. Brush the edges of the pastry with beaten egg, fold over the pastry, and seal the edges well. Cut each one into four sausage rolls and place them, cut-side down, on a baking sheet. Brush with beaten egg and make three diagonal slits on the top of each sausage roll. Bake for 25 minutes. Serve hot or cold.

Maids of Honour

These little cakes were originally made in the kitchens of Richmond Palace and were named by Henry VIII in honour of the girls who attended the queen of the moment.

The tart filling has to be prepared a day before it is needed.

Makes 12 tarts
Time Preparation 15 minutes, but start the preparation of the filling a day in advance, Baking 20 minutes
Oven Temperature Gas Mark 7/220°C/425°F

Ingredients
Filling

600 ml (1 pint) milk	1 egg
50 g (2 oz) sugar	1 tablespoon brandy
1 teaspoon junket rennet	25 g (1 oz) ground almonds
75 g (3 oz) unsalted butter	

250 g (8 oz) made puff pastry (p. 68)

Method
Put the milk and half the sugar into a pan and heat gently until just warm, but not hot. Remove from the heat and stir in the rennet. Leave in the pan for 30 minutes. Pour into a very fine sieve over a bowl and leave in a cool place overnight.

Cream the butter with the remaining sugar, and work in the curds which have formed in the sieve. Beat in the egg, brandy and almonds.

Line 12 deep tartlet tins with the pastry. Spoon in the filling. Bake for 20 minutes and cool on a wire rack.

Summer Fruit Tarts

For these tarts, crisp pastry cases are filled with a delicious mixture of raspberries and redcurrants topped with whipped cream, and they look beautiful on a buffet table.

Makes 18 tarts
Time Preparation 20 minutes, Baking 10 minutes
Oven Temperature Gas Mark 6/200°C/400°F

Ingredients
350 g (12 oz) made shortcrust pastry (p. 66)

Filling

250 g (8 oz) redcurrants	2 tablespoons cornflour
125 g (4 oz) raspberries	2 tablespoons cold water
250 g (8 oz) caster sugar	

Topping

150 g (¼ pint) double cream	1 teaspoon icing sugar

Method
Roll out the pastry and use it to line 18 tart tins. Prick the pastry cases well with a fork and bake blind for 10 minutes. Lift on to a wire rack to cool.

Mix together the redcurrants and raspberries in a pan and stir in the sugar. Cook gently over a low heat for 10 minutes. Mix together the cornflour and water and stir into the fruit. Continue stirring over a low heat until the mixture is thick and clear. Chill the filling.

Just before serving, spoon the filling into the pastry cases. Whip the cream and icing sugar, and pipe in whorls on top of the filling.

Cumberland Currant Slice

From the seventeenth century onwards, north-west England had many ports to which sugar and rum were imported from the West Indies. Smuggling was rife, and rum became a popular flavouring for local dishes.

Makes 9 slices
Time Preparation 15 minutes, Baking 40 minutes
Oven Temperature Gas Mark 6/200°C/400°F, *then* Gas Mark 4/180°C/350°F

Ingredients
350 g (12 oz) made shortcrust pastry (p. 66)

Filling

175 g (6 oz) currants	½ teaspoon ground allspice
50 g (2 oz) butter	¼ teaspoon ground cinnamon
50 g (2 oz) dark soft brown sugar	pinch of ground mace
grated rind of 1 lemon	2 tablespoons dark rum

Method
Lightly grease a shallow 20 cm (8 in) square tin. Roll out the pastry, and use half of it to line the tin.

Put the currants, butter, sugar, lemon rind and spices into a pan and heat gently until the butter has melted. Remove from the heat, stir well and leave to cool. Stir in the rum. Spread the cold filling in the pastry case.

Cover the filling with the second piece of pastry, and seal the edges by pinching with the fingers. Prick the surface lightly with a fork. Bake at the higher oven temperature for 10 minutes. Reduce the heat and continue baking for 30 minutes. Cool in the tin, and cut into squares. Serve as a cake, or with cream or custard.

Top Cumberland Currant Slice; *Bottom* Maids of Honour

Strawberry Hearts

Crisp little pastry hearts are sandwiched together with jam and cream. In the summer, sliced strawberries may be used instead of the jam.

Makes 10 hearts
Time Preparation 15 minutes, Baking 10 minutes
Oven Temperature Gas Mark 7/220°C/425°F

Ingredients
350 g (12 oz) made puff
   pastry (p. 68)
50 g (2 oz) caster sugar
150 ml (¼ pint) double
   cream

4 tablespoons strawberry
   jam

Method
Roll out the pastry into a rectangle 45 cm × 25 cm (18 in × 10 in). Sprinkle with one-third of the sugar. Fold the short ends in to meet in the middle and press them down firmly. Sprinkle again with one-third of the sugar and fold the ends to the centre again. Sprinkle with the remaining sugar, and fold the pastry in half, so that the two folded portions are together. Press down well and cut into slices, each about 1.25 cm (½ in) wide.

Place the slices on a baking sheet which has been rinsed in cold water but not dried, leaving room for spreading. Bake for 5 minutes until golden-brown. Turn over and bake for a further 5 minutes. Cool on a wire rack.

Whip the cream to stiff peaks. Spread the jam on half the hearts. Spread cream over the jam and top with the remaining hearts.

Apple Strudel

Apple Strudel is a favourite Austrian pastry which takes a little care in making, but which looks and tastes splendid.

Makes 1 large strudel
Time Preparation 20 minutes, Resting 1 hour, Baking 30 minutes
Oven Temperature Gas Mark 7/220°C/425°F

Ingredients
250 g (8 oz) plain flour
pinch of salt
1 egg

1 tablespoon oil
6 tablespoons tepid water

Filling
500 g (1 lb) eating apples,
   peeled, cored and sliced
   thinly
50 g (2 oz) chopped walnuts
50 g (2 oz) currants or
   sultanas
2 teaspoons ground mixed
   spice

50–75 g (2–3 oz) light soft
   brown sugar
65 g (2½ oz) butter
2 tablespoons fresh white
   breadcrumbs

icing sugar, for sprinkling

Method
Sieve the flour and salt into a bowl, and drop the egg into the centre. Mix the oil and water and add to the bowl, and work the ingredients together to make a smooth dough. Knead the dough on a lightly floured board until it is smooth and elastic. Cover it with a cloth, and leave to rest for 1 hour.

Mix the apple slices with the nuts, dried fruit, spice and sugar. Melt 25 g (1 oz) butter and fry the breadcrumbs until golden-brown.

Put a clean cloth on the table and flour it lightly. Roll out the dough on the cloth, then pull and stretch the dough over the backs of the hands until it is thin and transparent. Trim off any thick edges. Melt the remaining butter and brush over the surface of the pastry. Sprinkle with breadcrumbs and then spread the apple mixture evenly over the top.

Lifting the cloth by the two nearside corners, roll up the dough into a long, thin sausage. Bend into a horseshoe shape and place on a lightly greased baking sheet. Brush with any remaining butter. Bake for 30 minutes, until crisp and golden-brown.

Sprinkle thickly with icing sugar, and serve hot or cold, in slices.

Top May Day Tarts; *Bottom*
Clifton Puffs (p. 76)

May Day Tarts

These little iced tarts have a delicate hint of almonds or rosewater and are perfect for teatime.

Makes 12 tarts
Time Preparation 20 minutes, Baking 22 minutes
Oven Temperature Gas Mark 6/200°C/400°F, *then* Gas Mark 4/180°C/350°F

Ingredients
175 g (6 oz) made shortcrust pastry (p. 66)

Filling
50 g (2 oz) unsalted butter
50 g (2 oz) caster sugar
1 egg, beaten
50 g (2 oz) currants
25 g (1 oz) ground almonds

25 g (1 oz) mixed candied peel, chopped
½ teaspoon almond essence or rosewater

Icing
juice of 1 lemon

75 g (3 oz) icing sugar

Method
Roll out the pastry and line 12 tart tins. Reserve the pastry trimmings.

Cream the butter with the sugar until they are light and fluffy, and then work in the egg. Stir in the currants, almonds, candied peel and almond essence or rosewater.

Spoon the filling into the pastry cases. Roll out the pastry trimmings, cut into strips and use to form a cross or lattice on top of the filling. Bake at the higher oven temperature for 7 minutes. Reduce the heat and continue baking for 15 minutes. Lift the tarts on to a wire rack and set aside.

Mix the lemon juice and icing sugar until smooth. While the tarts are still warm, spoon the icing over the top of each tart. Alternatively, sprinkle with a light dusting of icing sugar.

Clifton Puffs

These puffy triangles are filled with dried fruit and nuts and have a subtle flavour of almonds and nutmeg.

Makes 10 puffs
Time Preparation 20 minutes, Baking 25 minutes
Oven Temperature Gas Mark 7/220°C/425°F

Ingredients

500 g (1 lb) made puff pastry (p. 68)
25 g (1 oz) ground almonds

1 teaspoon caster sugar

Filling

125 g (4 oz) eating apples, peeled and finely chopped
125 g (4 oz) currants
125 g (4 oz) blanched almonds, chopped

50 g (2 oz) seedless raisins
50 g (2 oz) mixed candied peel, chopped
1 tablespoon brandy
¼ teaspoon ground nutmeg

milk and caster sugar, for glazing

Method

Roll out the pastry on a board sprinkled with ground almonds and caster sugar. Fold the pastry in three and roll it out again thinly. Cut into ten × 10 cm (4 in) squares.

Mix the chopped apple with the currants, almonds, raisins, candied peel, brandy and nutmeg. Divide the mixture between the pastry squares, placing it in the centre of each square. Fold the pastry over to form triangles, dampen the edges with water and seal firmly.

Rinse the two baking sheets in cold water but do not dry them. Place the pastry triangles on the baking sheets, brush with milk and sprinkle with caster sugar. Bake for 25 minutes. Serve warm and freshly baked.

Apple Crisps

An attractive variation on the apple pie theme, the eating apples in this recipe retain their shape. Serve with cream or ice cream.

Makes 10 pieces
Time Preparation 15 minutes, Baking 30 minutes
Oven Temperature Gas Mark 7/220°C/425°F, *then* Gas Mark 4/180°C/350°F

Ingredients

350 g (12 oz) made shortcrust pastry (p. 66)
5 tablespoons soft white breadcrumbs
6 tablespoons apricot jam

500 g (1 lb) crisp eating apples, peeled, cored and quartered

Method

Roll out the pastry and use it to line a lightly greased 25 cm × 20 cm (10 in × 8 in) tin. Sprinkle with half the breadcrumbs. Warm the jam and sprinkle half of it over the breadcrumbs.

Cut the apple quarters into neat, thin slices and arrange these in lines on the pastry. Brush with the remaining jam, and scatter on the remaining crumbs.

Bake for 20 minutes at the higher oven temperature, then reduce the temperature and continue baking for 10 minutes. Serve hot or cold.

Top Game Pie (p. 83); *Bottom* Classic Quiche Lorraine (p. 82)

Pies and flans

*T*he varieties of pastry described in
the previous chapter may be used for pies made in deep dishes and for
plate pies, as well as for open quiches, tarts and flans.

Covering a Pie Dish

Roll out the pastry about 5 cm (2 in) larger than the pie dish.
Dampen the edge of the pie dish with water, and cut a strip
of pastry a little wider than the edge to place on top. Put on
the pastry strip and brush with a little beaten egg. Cover
with the remaining pastry as a lid, and press the edges
lightly together. Trim the edges with a sharp knife, held at a
slight angle away from the dish, and cut in short, clean
strokes. Tap the edge sharply at intervals with the back of a
knife to seal and give a neat edge. (This is known as
'knocking up'.) To flute edges, press a thumb on the top
outer edge and, with the back of a knife, draw the edge
towards the centre of the pie for 1.25 cm (½ in) all round the
edge. On a savoury pie, there should be about 1.75 cm (¾ in)
between cuts; on a sweet pie the gap should be about 0.75
cm (¼ in). The edges may also be pressed with a fork with
the prongs pointing inwards, or the edges may be pinched
between thumb and first finger. A small hole or two slits
should be cut on the surface to release steam.

Glazing a Pie

For savoury pies, brush the top evenly with beaten egg, or a
mixture of egg and milk or egg and water, using a whole egg
or only egg yolks. A pinch of salt sprinkled over the top will
make the glaze very shiny.

For sweet pies, brush the top with milk or water and
sprinkle with caster sugar before baking. If preferred, egg
white can be used and sprinkled with caster sugar 7–10
minutes before the end of baking.

Lining a Flan Ring

Only metal flan rings or flan tins should be used as they
conduct heat quickly to the pastry. A plain flan ring is a
metal hoop placed on a baking sheet without a rim so that
the finished flan may be slipped easily on to a serving plate.
A flan tin may be used alone, although it is safer to place it
on a baking sheet in case the filling leaks. If a flan tin has a
removable base, it is very easy to unmould the pastry when

Use a pastry lid to cover a pie
dish.

Line a metal tin by gently
pressing the pastry into the sides
and base.

Flute the edges of a pastry lid
using the thumb and back of a
knife.

cooked. Traditionally, savoury flans should be baked in plain tins, and sweet ones in fluted tins.

Put the flan ring on to a baking sheet, or the flan tin on to a firm surface. Roll out the pastry to a circle about 5 cm (2 in) larger than the container to be used. Lift the pastry by loosely rolling it round the rolling pin, or by folding the pastry into quarters. Lift gently into the container and unroll or unfold. Ease the pastry carefully into shape, without pulling or stretching it. Starting in the middle, work towards the sides of the container, pushing out air from under the base. Gently press the pastry into the sides of the tin with the back of a finger, being careful not to crack or tear the pastry. Roll firmly across the top with a rolling pin to cut off surplus pastry. Place the prepared flan on a baking sheet which has been heated in the oven; this helps to seal the base firmly and make it crisp. For details of baking an empty flan case see 'Baking Blind' on page 18.

Glazing Fruit Tarts

A sweet tart looks and tastes delicious if finished with a jam glaze. A yellow glaze made from apricot jam should be used for white, orange or green fruit. A red glaze made from raspberry jam or redcurrant jelly should be used for red, purple and pink fruit.

To make *Apricot Glaze*, add 4 tablespoons warm water and the juice of ½ lemon to 500 g (1 lb) apricot jam. Bring slowly to the boil, simmer for 5 minutes and sieve. Return to the pan and boil for 5 minutes, and brush on the fruit while warm. This glaze may be stored in a jam jar, ready for use when required. *Raspberry Glaze* is made in the same way. For *Redcurrant Glaze*, beat some redcurrant jelly until well broken up. Strain it into a pan and heat it gently, without stirring, until it is clear; do not boil. Brush the glaze over the fruit while it is warm.

Tomato and Onion Flan

This savoury flan is full of flavour and particularly good for a summer day. The eggs are optional, but they help to make an easy-to-serve and substantial meal.

Makes 1 flan
Time Preparation 40 minutes, Baking 20 minutes
Oven Temperature Gas Mark 6/200°C/400°F

Ingredients
350 g (12 oz) made shortcrust pastry (p. 66)

Filling
500 g (1 lb) onions, chopped finely	sprig of thyme
2 garlic cloves, chopped finely or crushed	1 bay leaf
5 tablespoons olive oil	salt and pepper
1 kg (2 lb) ripe tomatoes, chopped roughly	6 eggs, poached lightly (optional)

Method
Roll out the pastry and use it to line a 22.5 cm (9 in) flan tin. Prick the base lightly, line it with greaseproof paper and baking beans, and bake blind for 15 minutes. Remove the paper and beans, and continue baking for 5 minutes.

While the pastry is baking, prepare the filling. Put the onions and garlic into a pan with half the oil, and simmer for 25 minutes, until the onions are very soft. Cook the tomatoes in another pan with the remaining oil, thyme and bay leaf, until they form a thick purée. Put the onions and tomatoes through a sieve and mix well together. Season with salt and pepper, and pour into the pastry case. If liked, arrange poached eggs on top. Serve at once.

Blue Cheese Quiche

A tangy mixture of blue cheese and onions makes an unusual filling for a crisp pastry case.

Makes 1 quiche
Time Preparation 20 minutes, Baking 35 minutes
Oven Temperature Gas Mark 7/220°C/425°F, *then* Gas Mark 4/180°C/350°F

Ingredients
250 g (8 oz) made shortcrust pastry (p. 66)

Filling
75 g (3 oz) butter	300 ml (½ pint) milk
250 g (8 oz) onions, sliced thinly	pinch of mustard powder
salt and pepper	125 g (4 oz) blue cheese, crumbled
40 g (1½ oz) plain flour	

Method
Roll out the pastry and use it to line a 20 cm (8 in) flan ring.

Melt 50 g (2 oz) butter in a pan, and cook the onions very gently until they are soft and golden. Season well with salt and pepper. Put into a bowl.

In the pan, melt the remaining butter, work in the flour, and cook for 1 minute. Stir in the milk and cook over a low heat until the sauce is smooth and creamy. Season with mustard powder. Take off the heat, and stir in the onions and cheese. Put into the pastry case and bake at the higher oven temperature for 15 minutes. Reduce the heat to the lower temperature, and continue baking for 20 minutes.

Steak, Kidney and Mushroom Pie

The thick, succulent filling of this traditional favourite contrasts with the crisp pastry.

Makes 1 pie
Time Preparation 20 minutes, Simmering 1½–2 hours, Baking 35 minutes
Oven Temperature Gas Mark 7/220°C/425°F, *then* Gas Mark 4/180°C/350°F

Ingredients
Filling
750 g (1½ lb) stewing steak
250 g (8 oz) ox kidney
25 g (1 oz) seasoned flour
25 g (1 oz) lard
1 medium onion, chopped finely

125 g (4 oz) button mushrooms, halved
300 ml (½ pint) beef stock

250 g (8 oz) made puff pastry (p. 68)

beaten egg, for glazing

Method
Cut the steak and kidney into neat cubes and toss in the flour until lightly coated. Reserve any surplus flour. Melt the lard, and cook the onion until it is just soft and golden. Add the meat and brown quickly on all sides. Add the mushrooms and cook for 1 minute. Sprinkle in the reserved flour and stir in the stock. Bring to the boil, cover and simmer for 1½–2 hours, until the meat is tender. Put into a 900 ml (1½ pint) pie dish and leave until cold.

Roll out the pastry so that it is 2.5 cm (1 in) larger than the top of the pie dish. Cut off a strip of pastry about 1.25 cm (½ in) wide to fit the rim of the dish. Moisten the dish rim and press on the pastry strip. Moisten the strip lightly and carefully put on the pastry lid. Press down well to seal the edges and then flute them. Brush well with beaten egg to glaze.

Place the pie dish on a baking sheet. Bake at the higher oven temperature for 20 minutes. Reduce the oven temperature, and continue baking for 15 minutes.

Classic Quiche Lorraine

The authentic Quiche Lorraine is very simple but very rich, and is best eaten hot, as it is made with puff pastry.

Makes 1 quiche
Time Preparation 20 minutes, Baking 40 minutes
Oven Temperature Gas Mark 7/220°C/425°F, *then* Gas Mark 5/190°C/375°F

Ingredients
350 g (12 oz) made puff pastry (p. 68)

Filling
125 g (4 oz) unsmoked bacon, diced
75 g (3 oz) cooked ham, chopped
4 eggs, beaten lightly

600 ml (1 pint) single cream
50 g (2 oz) butter, cut into flakes
pepper

Method
Roll out the pastry and use it to line a 22.5 cm (9 in) flan ring. Prick the pastry base very lightly with the point of a knife.

Put the bacon into a pan and just cover with water. Simmer for 15 minutes and then drain very well. Mix the ham with the bacon and sprinkle in the pastry case. Mix together the eggs, cream and flakes of butter. Season with pepper and pour over the bacon and ham in the pastry case.

Bake at the higher oven temperature for 10 minutes. Reduce the heat to the lower temperature, and continue baking for 30 minutes.

Fisherman's Puff

This is rather like a large vol-au-vent and it is delicious with vegetables or a green salad.

Makes 1 puff
Time Preparation 20 minutes, Baking 20 minutes
Oven Temperature Gas Mark 7/220°C/425°F

Ingredients
500 g (1 lb) made puff pastry (p. 68)
beaten egg, for glazing

Filling
40 g (1½ oz) butter
40 g (1½ oz) plain flour
300 ml (½ pint) dry cider
150 ml (¼ pint) milk
500 g (1 lb) smoked haddock fillet

3 eggs, hard-boiled and chopped finely
125 g (4 oz) cooked peas
salt and pepper
few drops of Tabasco sauce

Method
Roll out the pastry into a 27.5 cm × 20 cm (11 in × 8 in) rectangle. With a knife, mark out a rectangle 2.5 cm (1 in) from the edge, without cutting right through the pastry, so that a 'lid' will be formed. Brush with egg to glaze and bake for 20 minutes. Remove the lid carefully from the pastry case.

While the pastry is cooking, prepare the filling. Melt the butter in a pan, work in the flour, and cook for 1 minute. Remove from the heat and gradually stir in the cider and milk. Return to the heat and bring to the boil, stirring all the time. Cook for 1 minute, and then take off the heat again.

Poach the haddock until just tender, and break the fish into flakes. Stir the fish, eggs and peas into the sauce, and season with salt, pepper and Tabasco sauce. Pour the filling into the pastry case and replace the lid before serving.

Game Pie

Instead of the pheasant, other game such as grouse, partridge or pigeons may be used. If venison is available, this can be used instead of the steak. Pieces of hare and/or rabbit may also be included. A total of about 625 g (1¼ lb) mixed meat and game is needed in addition to the sausagemeat and bacon.

Makes 1 game pie
Time Preparation 30 minutes (plus standing and setting time), Baking 1½ hours
Oven Temperature Gas Mark 7/220°C/425°F, *then* Gas Mark 5/190°C/375°F, *then* Gas Mark 4/180°C/350°F

Ingredients
Hot Water Pastry
250 g (8 oz) plain flour
250 g (8 oz) plain wholemeal flour
1 teaspoon salt

150 g (5 oz) lard
150 ml (¼ pint) milk and water mixed

Filling
350 g (12 oz) pork sausagemeat
125 g (4 oz) lean bacon
175 g (6 oz) lean chuck steak
1 pheasant or other game bird

salt and pepper
150–300 ml (¼–½ pint) jellied stock

beaten egg, for glazing

Method
Before making the pie, start preparations for the jellied stock. This is made using the trimmings from the meat and game, including bones, which are just covered with water and simmered for 1½ hours, before straining and chilling. If preferred, chicken stock may be made from a stock cube, with 2 teaspoons powdered gelatine added before cooling.

To make the pastry, sieve the flours and salt into a warm bowl. Put the lard, milk and water into a pan, and heat until the fat melts. Bring to the boil and pour at once into the centre of the flour. Mix with a wooden spoon to form a paste. Turn on to a lightly floured board and knead quickly until smooth. Lightly grease an oval, hinged game pie tin or a 17.5 cm (7 in) round cake tin with removable base. Use three-quarters of the pastry to line the tin, pressing the pastry well into the sides.

Line the pastry with a thin layer of sausagemeat. Cut the bacon and steak into small cubes. Strip the flesh from the game bird and cut into small pieces. Mix the meats together well and season with salt and pepper. Add about 4 tablespoons of the stock and pack the meat into the pastry case. Cover with the remaining pastry and decorate with pastry leaves. Make a hole in the centre of the pastry lid, and brush the lid lightly with beaten egg.

Bake for 30 minutes at the highest oven temperature given above. Lower the temperature, and continue baking for 30 minutes. Brush again with egg glaze, reduce the heat a second time, and continue baking for 30 minutes.

Remove the pie from the oven and leave to stand for 45 minutes. Warm the stock and gently spoon into the hole in the top. (If this is difficult, use a little funnel made of foil.) Leave in a cold place for at least 12 hours, until the pie is completely cold and set. Remove from the tin and place on a serving dish.

Norfolk Apple Pie

Norfolk Apple Pie

Marmalade and dried fruit give a very special flavour to this double-crust apple pie.

Makes 1 pie
Time Preparation 30 minutes, Baking 45 minutes
Oven Temperature Gas Mark 6/200°C/400°F, *then* Gas Mark 4/180°C/350°F

Ingredients
500 g (1 lb) made shortcrust pastry (p. 66)

Filling
1 kg (2 lb) cooking apples, peeled and cored
50 g (2 oz) butter
125 g (4 oz) sugar

2 tablespoons orange marmalade
2 tablespoons currants

caster sugar, for sprinkling

Method
Roll out the pastry and use half of it to line a 22.5 cm (9 in) pie plate. Slice the apples into a pan, and cook over a very low heat, without water, until the apples start to break up. Add the butter and continue cooking until the apples are fluffy. Remove from the heat and stir in the sugar, marmalade and currants. Leave until cold.

Put the apple filling into the pastry case, cover with the remaining pastry, and seal the edges well. Bake at the higher oven temperature for 25 minutes, then reduce the heat to the lower temperature and continue baking for 20 minutes. Sprinkle with sugar and serve hot.

Top Autumn Fruit Pie; *Bottom* Orange Cream Tart

Autumn Fruit Pie

A mixture of fruit gives this pie a lovely flavour and is a good way of using small quantities of different fruit.

Makes 1 pie
Time Preparation 15 minutes, Baking 25 minutes
Oven Temperature Gas Mark 7/220°C/425°F

Ingredients
350 g (12 oz) made puff pastry (p. 68)

Filling
350 g (12 oz) plums, halved   250 g (8 oz) blackberries
250 g (8 oz) cooking apples,   175 g (6 oz) sugar
  peeled, cored and sliced   8 tablespoons water
250 g (8 oz) eating pears,
  peeled, cored and cubed

milk, for glazing
caster sugar, for sprinkling

Method
Roll out the pastry to cover a 900 ml (1½ pint) pie dish. Put the plums into a saucepan, and add the apples and pears with the blackberries and sugar. Add water and simmer for 10 minutes. Leave until cold.

Put the fruit into the pie dish and cover with the pastry. Brush the pastry with a little milk to glaze it, and bake for 25 minutes. Sprinkle with caster sugar before serving.

Orange Cream Tart

This is a richly flavoured orange tart which should be served freshly made.

Makes 1 × 20 cm (8 in) tart
Time Preparation 40 minutes (plus chilling time), Baking 20 minutes
Oven Temperature Gas Mark 6/200°C/400°F

Ingredients
250 g (8 oz) made sweet shortcrust pastry (p. 67)

Filling
2 egg yolks   2 thin-skinned oranges
50 g (2 oz) caster sugar   3 tablespoons orange jelly
25 g (1 oz) plain flour   marmalade
300 ml (½ pint) creamy   2 teaspoons orange liqueur
  milk

Method
Roll out the pastry and line a 20 cm (8 in) flan tin with it. Line with greaseproof paper and fill with baking beans, and bake blind for 15 minutes. Remove the paper and beans, and continue baking for 5 minutes, until the pastry is dry, crisp and lightly golden. Leave until cold.

Mix together the egg yolks, sugar and flour. Put the milk into a pan and heat to just below boiling point, and pour on to the egg yolks. Mix well, and return the mixture to the pan. Grate the rind from one of the oranges and add it to the egg mixture. Stir over a low heat for 3 minutes, until smooth and creamy. Leave until cool and spread in the baked pastry case. Chill for 30 minutes.

Peel the oranges and remove all the white pith. Slice the fruit in thin, crosswise slices and arrange on top of the custard. Warm the marmalade until just liquid and stir in the liqueur. Brush over the orange slices. Serve freshly made.

Top Sailor Hats (p. 92); *Centre* Walnut Chocolate Circles (p. 92); *Bottom* Viennese Biscuits (p. 92)

Biscuits and cookies

H

ome-made biscuits look very attractive and are delicious to eat. They are quick and easy to make, and a large batch of biscuits results from a small batch of dough which is economical to prepare. There are five main types of biscuit, and those cooks who are short of time will find that tray biscuits and drop biscuits are the quickest to make. These give a slightly more cake-like result than other biscuits, and they are generally known as cookies.

Tray biscuits are prepared from soft dough which is pressed into a shallow square or rectangular tin. The outlines of the biscuits are marked lightly on the warm, cooked dough; they are then cut into pieces and removed from the tin when cold.

Drop biscuits are also made from soft dough, which is either dropped in rough spoonfuls on baking sheets, or rolled lightly into small balls about the size of a walnut before being placed on the baking sheets. These biscuits tend to spread in the oven, but their shapes can be made neater if the biscuits are slightly flattened with a wide-bladed knife or fork dipped in cold water just before they are cooked.

Piped biscuits look very professional, but they are quite difficult to shape neatly. The dough should be of a firm piping consistency, and may be piped from an icing bag or a special metal biscuit tube.

Rolled and cut biscuits are made from firm dough, rolled out thinly and cut into shapes with metal cutters. Larger biscuits may be cut with the rim of a large drinking glass. These biscuits may be pricked lightly with a fork before baking to give an attractive finish.

Chilled and cut biscuits are made from a firm dough, formed into a cylinder and chilled in the refrigerator or freezer. Slices may be cut from the dough and baked, even straight from the freezer.

Baking Hints

Biscuits are baked in a moderate oven for 10–15 minutes. They should not be allowed to overcook or become dark brown; the perfect biscuit is pale gold in colour. Biscuits containing honey or golden syrup darken quickly and should be timed carefully, and inspected a few minutes before the recommended cooking time is completed.

Flatten spoonfuls of dough for drop biscuits with a fork dipped in cold water.

Use a piping bag to make different shapes for piped biscuits.

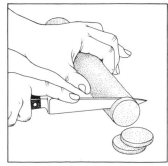

Cut slices from a cylinder of dough to make chilled and cut biscuits.

Biscuits are soft when taken from the oven heat. It is best to leave them on the baking sheet for a few seconds to firm up, and then to lift them carefully with a palette knife on to a wire rack, so that they become cold and crisp. An attractive finish may be given with a dusting of caster sugar on the surface of each biscuit, or pairs of biscuits may be sandwiched with jam or butter icing. Biscuits are best stored in airtight tins or storage boxes, or they lose their essential crispness.

Top Lemon Crisps; *Bottom* Chocolate Butter Rings

Easter Biscuits

Traditionally eaten at Easter, these biscuits may be flavoured with currants, although caraway seeds were the original flavouring.

Makes 36 biscuits
Time Preparation 15 minutes, Baking 15 minutes
Oven Temperature Gas Mark 4/180°C/350°F

Ingredients

250 g (8 oz) plain flour	pinch of ground nutmeg
250 g (8 oz) caster sugar	2 eggs
250 g (8 oz) butter, cut into pieces	2 tablespoons dry sherry
50 g (2 oz) currants *or* 7 g (¼ oz) caraway seeds	2 tablespoons rosewater

Method
Sieve the flour into a bowl and stir in the sugar until evenly mixed. Rub in the butter until the mixture is like fine breadcrumbs. Stir in the currants or caraway seeds, and add the nutmeg. Beat the eggs, sherry and rosewater together lightly, and work into the dry ingredients to make a firm, soft dough.

Grease and flour two baking sheets. Roll out the dough thinly and cut into 5 cm (2 in) circles with a plain or fluted cutter. Put on to the baking sheets and prick each biscuit lightly six times with a fork. Bake for 15 minutes, and cool on a wire rack.

Chocolate Butter Rings

These are simple chocolate biscuits, sandwiched together with apricot or raspberry jam or lemon curd. If preferred, they may be sandwiched with chocolate or coffee buttercream.

Makes 24 biscuits
Time Preparation 15 minutes, Baking 10 minutes
Oven Temperature Gas Mark 6/200°C/400°F

Ingredients

250 g (8 oz) butter	6 tablespoons apricot or raspberry jam, or lemon curd
125 g (4 oz) caster sugar	
350 g (12 oz) plain flour	
50 g (2 oz) cocoa	icing sugar, for sprinkling
pinch of salt	

Method
Cream the butter and sugar together until light and fluffy. Sieve the flour, cocoa and salt together, and then work these dry ingredients into the creamed mixture to make a firm dough.

Roll out the dough on a lightly floured board and cut into 5 cm (2 in) rounds with a plain cutter. Cut out the centre of half the biscuits with a 2.5 cm (1 in) cutter. Place on two greased baking sheets, and bake for 10 minutes. Lift carefully on to a wire rack to cool.

Spread jam or lemon curd on the whole biscuits, piling it a little higher in the centre. Press on the biscuits rings firmly, and sprinkle with icing sugar.

Lemon Crisps

These crunchy biscuits with a light lemon flavour are delicious served with mousses or fruit.

Makes 24 biscuits
Time Preparation 15 minutes, Baking 12 minutes
Oven Temperature Gas Mark 4/180°C/350°F

Ingredients

125 g (4 oz) plain flour	grated rind of 1 lemon
40 g (1½ oz) butter or hard margarine, cut into pieces	few drops of lemon essence
50 g (2 oz) porridge oats	2 tablespoons golden syrup
40 g (1½ oz) caster sugar	2–3 tablespoons milk

Method
Sieve the flour into a bowl, and rub in the fat until the mixture resembles fine breadcrumbs. Stir in the oats, sugar and lemon rind until evenly mixed. Add the essence, syrup and enough milk to make a stiff dough.

Roll out the dough on a lightly floured board and cut into 5 cm (2 in) rounds with a plain cutter. Place on two lightly greased baking sheets, and bake for 12 minutes. Lift carefully on to a wire rack to cool.

Top Gingerbread Men; *Bottom* Macaroons

Gingerbread Men

Children love little men made from crisp gingerbread with currant features and buttons, but the same mixture may be cut into other shapes if preferred.

Makes 24 biscuits
Time Preparation 20 minutes, Baking 15 minutes
Oven Temperature Gas Mark 4/180°C/350°F

Ingredients

250 g (8 oz) plain flour	25 g (1 oz) sugar
pinch of salt	2 tablespoons black treacle
2 teaspoons ground ginger	1 egg yolk
150 g (5 oz) butter or hard margarine, cut into pieces	

Topping and Decoration

1 egg white	currants
25 g (1 oz) caster sugar	

Method

Sieve the flour, salt and ginger into a bowl, and rub in the fat until the mixture is like fine breadcrumbs. Stir in the sugar. Mix together the treacle and egg yolk, and work them into the flour to make a stiff dough.

Roll out the dough on a lightly floured board, and cut into shapes with a gingerbread man cutter. Place on two lightly greased baking sheets. Lightly beat the egg white and brush this over the biscuits. Sprinkle with sugar, and mark eyes, mouth and buttons with currants.

Bake for 15 minutes, and lift on to a wire rack to cool.

Bosworth Jumbles

The recipe for these delicacies was supposedly found on Bosworth Field at the end of the Wars of the Roses. The name derives from the old French word for an entwined ring for lovers.

Makes 24 biscuits
Time Preparation 10 minutes, Baking 12 minutes
Oven Temperature Gas Mark 4/180°C/350°F

Ingredients

150 g (5 oz) unsalted butter	50 g (2 oz) ground almonds
150 g (5 oz) caster sugar	1 teaspoon grated lemon rind
1 egg	
300 g (10 oz) plain flour	pinch of ground ginger

Method

Cream the butter and sugar together until light and fluffy, and work in the egg with a little flour. Add the remaining flour, almonds, lemon rind and ginger to make a soft but firm dough.

On a lightly floured board, roll the mixture with the hands into sausage-shaped pieces about the thickness of a middle finger. Cut off pieces 12.5 cm (5 in) long. Grease two baking sheets lightly. Put on the biscuits, curving them into 'S' shapes, and bake for 12 minutes. Lift carefully on to a wire rack to cool.

Macaroons

These almond biscuits were introduced from France at the beginning of the seventeenth century, and have remained popular for teatime, or to serve with fruit or ices.

Makes 18 macaroons
Time Preparation 15 minutes, Baking 20 minutes
Oven Temperature Gas Mark 4/180°C/350°F

Ingredients

2 egg whites	3 sheets rice paper
175 g (6 oz) ground almonds	18 blanched almonds
250 g (8 oz) caster sugar	

Method

Put the egg whites into a clean, dry and grease-free bowl. Whisk them until they stand in stiff peaks. Using a metal spoon, fold in the ground almonds and sugar until well blended.

Place the rice paper on three baking sheets. Put spoonfuls of the mixture on the rice paper, leaving room for them to spread. Place an almond on the centre of each.

Bake for 20 minutes. Carefully lift the rice paper on to a wire rack to cool. Trim off the surplus rice paper from each macaroon before serving.

Cornish Fairings

These nourishing and tasty biscuits come from the West Country, where they used to be sold at fairs and were taken home as presents.

Makes 24 biscuits
Time Preparation 10 minutes, Baking 15 minutes
Oven Temperature Gas Mark 4/180°C/350°F

Ingredients

125 g (4 oz) plain flour
pinch of salt
¼ teaspoon ground ginger
¼ teaspoon ground mixed spice
¼ teaspoon ground cinnamon
1½ teaspoons bicarbonate of soda

50 g (2 oz) butter, cut into pieces
50 g (2 oz) demerara sugar
2½ tablespoons golden syrup
25 g (1 oz) candied lemon peel, chopped finely

Method

Sift the flour, salt, spices and bicarbonate of soda into a bowl, and rub in the butter until the mixture is like fine breadcrumbs. Stir in the sugar. Warm the syrup until it runs easily, and pour it into the mixture. Work with the hands to form a soft dough, and then work in the lemon peel.

Take a rounded teaspoon of the mixture and roll between the hands to form a round ball or oval shape. Grease two baking sheets lightly. Put the balls of mixture on the baking sheets, allowing room for them to spread. Bake for 10 minutes.

Remove from the oven and hit each baking sheet firmly on a solid surface so that the fairings crack. Continue baking for 5 minutes. Leave on the baking sheets for 2 minutes, then lift on to a wire rack to cool.

Chocolate Sandwich Biscuits

These are crisp, dark chocolate biscuits, sandwiched with a creamy chocolate filling and sprinkled with crunchy sugar.

Makes 12 biscuits
Time Preparation 10 minutes, Baking 10 minutes
Oven Temperature Gas Mark 4/180°C/350°F

Ingredients

75 g (3 oz) plain flour
15 g (½ oz) cocoa powder
50 g (2 oz) butter or hard margarine

50 g (2 oz) caster sugar
1 egg yolk
¾ teaspoon vanilla essence
2 teaspoons water

Filling and Topping
75 g (3 oz) plain chocolate
15 g (½ oz) unsalted butter

2 teaspoons caster sugar

Method

Sift together the flour and cocoa. Cream the butter or margarine and sugar, and work in the egg yolk and vanilla essence. Add the flour mixture and water to make a stiff dough.

Roll out the dough thinly on a floured board and cut out 24 rectangles, about 7.5 cm × 2.5 cm (3 in × 1 in). Grease two baking sheets lightly. Put on the biscuits, and prick

each one four times with a fork. Bake for 10 minutes, and then cool on a wire rack.

To make the filling, break up the chocolate and put it into a bowl with the butter. Place the bowl over a pan of hot water and heat gently until the chocolate has melted. When the biscuits are cold, put them together in pairs with the chocolate filling. Leave until firm, and sprinkle the tops with caster sugar.

Petticoat Tails

Thin shortbread biscuits shaped like old-fashioned hooped petticoats, these are delicious with ice creams and fruit desserts.

Makes 9 biscuits
Time Preparation 10 minutes, Baking 20 minutes
Oven Temperature Gas Mark 4/180°C/350°F

Ingredients

300 g (10 oz) plain flour
50 g (2 oz) rice flour
150 g (5 oz) unsalted butter

4 tablespoons milk
50 g (2 oz) caster sugar
caster sugar, for sprinkling

Method

Sift the flours together into a bowl, and make a well in the middle. Put the butter and milk into a pan and heat until the butter has just melted. Pour into the well in the flour and add the sugar. Mix with the fingers and knead very lightly to a dough. Put on to a lightly floured board and roll into a circle about 1.75 cm (¾ in) thick.

Put an inverted dinner plate on top of the dough and cut round the edge with a sharp knife. Remove the dinner plate. Invert a wine glass in the centre of the round of dough and cut round this to make a small circle. Mark the remaining outer circle into eight segments, making a deep incision but not cutting right through the dough.

Grease a baking sheet lightly. Carefully lift the two pieces of dough on to the baking sheet, re-forming the circle. Bake for 20 minutes until golden. Cool on a wire rack, and reassemble the biscuits to form a large flat circle. Dust lightly with caster sugar before serving.

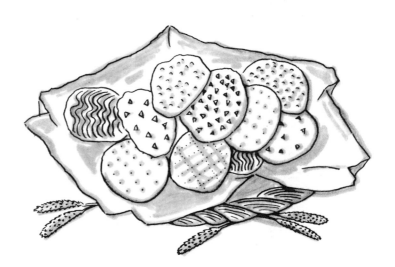

90   *Top left* Cornish Fairings (p. 89);
Top right Petticoat Tails (p. 89);
Bottom left Chocolate Sandwich
Biscuits (p. 89); *Bottom right*
Bosworth Jumbles (p. 88)

Viennese Biscuits

These biscuits are very short and light, and they look most attractive on the tea table. They are less rich if sandwiched with jam instead of chocolate filling.

Makes 12 biscuits
Time Preparation 20 minutes, Baking 15 minutes
Oven Temperature Gas Mark 3/160°C/325°F

Ingredients

125 g (4 oz) butter	1 small egg (size 4 or 5),
25 g (1 oz) icing sugar	beaten
125 g (4 oz) plain flour	½ teaspoon vanilla essence
25 g (1 oz) cornflour	

Filling

50 g (2 oz) plain chocolate, broken into pieces	250 g (8 oz) icing sugar
125 g (4 oz) butter, cut into small pieces	

icing sugar, for sprinkling

Method

Cream the butter and sugar together until light and fluffy. Work in the flour and cornflour. Mix in the egg and vanilla essence to give a dough of piping consistency.

Lightly grease two baking sheets. Put the mixture into a piping bag with a star nozzle. Pipe 7.5 cm (2 in) lengths on to the baking sheets, leaving room for the biscuits to spread slightly, and bake for 15 minutes. Lift on to a wire rack to cool.

To make the filling, melt the chocolate in a bowl over hot water. Remove from the heat, and beat the butter into the chocolate. Beat in the sugar gradually to make a soft cream. Sandwich the biscuits together in pairs. Sprinkle the tops with icing sugar.

Sailor Hats

These little biscuits were very popular in the 1930s, and they make an amusing talking point on the tea table. Children love them.

Makes 30 biscuits
Time Preparation 20 minutes, Baking 10 minutes
Oven Temperature Gas Mark 4/180°C/350°F

Ingredients

175 g (6 oz) self-raising flour	75 g (3 oz) caster sugar
50 g (2 oz) cornflour	1 egg, beaten
75 g (3 oz) butter	15 marshmallows

Icing and Decoration

175 g (6 oz) icing sugar	small sugar flowers or silver balls

Method

Sieve the flour and cornflour together. Cream the butter and sugar until light and fluffy. Add the egg and flour alternately, mixing well to form a light dough. Roll out the dough thinly on a lightly floured board and cut into 7.5 cm (3 in) rounds with a fluted cutter. Put on to two greased baking sheets, and bake for 10 minutes. Cool on a wire rack.

Cut the marshmallows in half horizontally to form 30 discs. Place a piece in the centre of each biscuit, cut-side down. Mix the icing sugar with enough water to make a creamy icing. Cover the marshmallows and biscuits with the icing and leave to set.

Decorate the top or round the crown of the 'hats' with sugar flowers or silver balls, or with a 'ribbon' of pink or blue icing.

Walnut Chocolate Circles

These are rather special biscuits, sandwiched with an unusual nutty filling and finished with chocolate icing.

Makes 20 biscuits
Time Preparation 20 minutes (plus cooling time), Baking 15 minutes
Oven Temperature Gas Mark 4/180°C/350°F

Ingredients

75 g (3 oz) plain chocolate	50 g (2 oz) caster sugar
2 tablespoons milk	½ teaspoon vanilla essence
250 g (8 oz) plain flour	1 egg yolk
175 g (6 oz) butter, cut into pieces	

Filling

3 tablespoons ground almonds	3 tablespoons apricot jam
1 tablespoon chopped walnuts	1 teaspoon orange juice

Icing

125 g (4 oz) icing sugar	2 tablespoons warm water
2 teaspoons cocoa	

Method

Put the chocolate and milk into a bowl over hot water and heat them until the chocolate has melted. Sieve the flour into a bowl and rub in the butter until the mixture is like fine breadcrumbs. Stir in the sugar and add the vanilla essence, egg yolk and chocolate. Mix to a smooth dough and leave until completely cold.

Roll out the dough on a lightly floured board and cut into 5 cm (2 in) rounds with a plain cutter. Put the biscuits on to two greased baking sheets, and bake for 15 minutes. Cool on a wire rack.

Prepare the filling by mixing together the ground almonds, walnuts, apricot jam and orange juice. Sandwich the biscuits together with the filling. Sieve the icing sugar into a bowl. Mix together the cocoa and water and work into the sugar. Spread the icing on top of the biscuits and leave to set.

Left Golf Biscuits; *Right* Cheese Thins

Golf Biscuits

These wholemeal biscuits may be eaten plain with a hot drink, but they are also very good served with cheese.

Makes 50 biscuits
Time Preparation 20 minutes, Baking 15 minutes
Oven Temperature Gas Mark 4/180°C/350°F

Ingredients

250 g (8 oz) plain wholemeal flour	125 g (4 oz) butter, cut into pieces
250 g (8 oz) fine oatmeal	125 g (4 oz) light soft brown sugar
pinch of salt	
1 teaspoon cream of tartar	1 egg
½ teaspoon ground cinnamon	2 tablespoons milk
¼ teaspoon bicarbonate of soda	

Method

Put the flour, oatmeal, salt, cream of tartar, cinnamon and bicarbonate of soda into a bowl, and stir together until evenly coloured. Rub in the butter until the mixture is like fine breadcrumbs. Stir in the sugar until evenly mixed. Beat the egg and milk together, and work into the mixture to make a soft, firm dough.

Roll out the dough thinly on a lightly floured board and cut into 5 cm (2 in) rounds or other shapes. Place on three lightly greased baking sheets and prick lightly with a fork. Bake for 15 minutes. Lift off carefully, and cool on a wire rack.

Cheese Thins

These simple biscuits are very good with drinks just as they are, or they may be spread with pâté or cream cheese.

Makes 36 biscuits
Time Preparation 15 minutes, Baking 10 minutes
Oven Temperature Gas Mark 5/190°C/375°F

Ingredients

125 g (4 oz) plain flour	½ teaspoon Worcestershire sauce
pinch of salt	sea salt, for sprinkling
pinch of mustard powder	
50 g (2 oz) butter	
50 g (2 oz) Cheddar cheese, grated	

Method

Sieve the flour, salt and mustard powder together. Cream the butter, cheese and Worcestershire sauce, and work in the flour to form a firm dough.

Roll out the dough thinly and cut into 5 cm (2 in) rounds or other shapes with a cutter. Place on two greased baking sheets, and bake for 10 minutes. Lift on to a wire rack, and sprinkle with sea salt while hot.

Shortbread

Try making this classic biscuit for Christmas, and tie it up with a tartan ribbon.

Makes 8 shortbread wedges
Time Preparation 10 minutes, Baking 35 minutes
Oven Temperature Gas Mark 3/160°C/325°F

Ingredients
200 g (7 oz) plain flour
25 g (1 oz) rice flour
125 g (4 oz) butter, cut into pieces
50 g (2 oz) caster sugar
caster sugar, for sprinkling

Method
Sieve the plain flour and rice flour together. Rub in the butter until the mixture is like fine breadcrumbs, and then stir in the sugar. Knead well to make a pliable dough.

Roll out the dough on a lightly floured board into a 17.5 cm (7 in) circle. Lift it on to a greased baking sheet, and mark it lightly into eight segments. Pinch the edges between finger and thumb, and prick the shortbread lightly with a fork.

Bake for 35 minutes until the shortbread is very pale gold in colour. Lift it carefully on a wire rack to cool. Sprinkle with sugar when cold.

Honey Flapjacks

This traditional favourite is made extra-special with a light flavouring of honey and ginger.

Makes 12 flapjacks
Time Preparation 5 minutes, Baking 25 minutes
Oven Temperature Gas Mark 4/180°C/350°F

Ingredients
150 g (5 oz) butter or hard margarine
75 g (3 oz) light soft brown sugar
2 tablespoons clear honey
250 g (8 oz) porridge oats
¼ teaspoon ground ginger

Method
Put the fat into a saucepan and heat it until just melted. Stir in all the other ingredients, mixing thoroughly.

Grease a 17.5 cm (7 in) square, shallow tin, press in the oat mixture, and bake for 25 minutes. While still hot, mark the flapjack into fingers with a sharp knife. Leave in the tin until cold. Cut the flapjack fingers through and lift out of the tin.

Refrigerator Biscuits

The dough for these biscuits may be prepared in advance and stored in the refrigerator for up to 3 days before baking.

Makes 24 biscuits
Time Preparation 15 minutes (plus chilling time), Baking 10 minutes
Oven Temperature Gas Mark 4/180°C/350°F

Ingredients
250 g (8 oz) butter
50 g (2 oz) caster sugar
1 teaspoon vanilla essence
350 g (12 oz) plain flour
15 g (½ oz) cocoa

Method
Cream together the butter and sugar until light and fluffy. Work in the vanilla essence and flour to make a soft but firm dough. Divide the dough in half. Add the cocoa to one half, mixing it in well until the dough is evenly coloured.

Shape each portion into a long roll, and cut each roll into two pieces. Put a plain roll and a chocolate roll next to each other, then arrange a chocolate roll on the plain one, and put the remaining plain roll on top of the chocolate one. Press them all together lightly, wrap in foil, and chill in the refrigerator.

To use, slice crosswise so that each biscuit consists of four circles, with two chocolate and two plain ones arranged diagonally. Put the biscuits on to two greased baking sheets, and bake for 10 minutes. Lift on to a wire rack to cool.

Top Chocolate Almond Cake
(p. 108); *Centre* Lemon Crust
Squares (p. 110); *Bottom* Sponge
Drops (p. 104)

Cakes

*E*veryday Cakes

CAKES FOR EVERYDAY family use are usually plain mixtures varied by the addition of dried fruit, spice or other flavouring. These cakes are made by the traditional creamed, rubbed-in and melted methods (pages 16–17) and take little time to assemble as they are made as a single layer and have no icing or filling. Because the cakes are so tempting, but not rich, they are often known as 'cut-and-come-again cakes'.

Mid-afternoon teatime was not invented until the 1840s, and early cakes were made to eat with a glass of Madeira, sherry or wine in the middle of the morning, since there was no midday meal, just one large meal each day which started in mid-afternoon and could go on for hours until the late evening. Cakes were then also served with tea at about 8 p.m. to finish off the day after the main meal. When luncheon became an established meal during the nineteenth century, these cakes were often served as 'luncheon cakes' after a main course, and it was traditional to eat fruit cake or gingerbread with a piece of farmhouse cheese.

Today, these cakes are, of course, useful for teatime, but once again our meal patterns are changing because of the greater demands of work and leisure, and so these plain cakes are just as good for a snack with coffee, as a filler for a lunch-box, or as an energy-giver for a sportsman.

Orange Walnut Cake

The refreshing flavour of this simple cake goes particularly well with a cup of coffee.

Makes 1 × 17.5 cm (7 in) cake
Time Preparation 10 minutes, Baking 1¼ hours
Oven Temperature Gas Mark 4/180°C/350°F

Ingredients
175 g (6 oz) butter
grated rind of 1 orange
175 g (6 oz) caster sugar
2 eggs, separated
300 g (10 oz) self-raising flour

50 g (2 oz) orange marmalade (medium-cut)
50 g (2 oz) candied orange peel, chopped
75 g (3 oz) walnuts, chopped
5 tablespoons water

Method
Cream the butter, orange rind and sugar together until light and fluffy. Sieve the flour. Beat the egg yolks into the creamed mixture one at a time with a teaspoonful of flour each time. Stir in the marmalade, candied peel, nuts and water and mix thoroughly. Fold in the remaining flour.

Whisk the egg whites until they form stiff peaks and fold them into the cake mixture. Grease a 17.5 cm (7 in) round cake tin and dust lightly with flour. Put in the mixture and bake for 1¼ hours. Cool in the tin for 5 minutes before turning on to a wire rack to cool completely.

Colchester Gingerbread

This gingerbread used to be eaten with a glass of gin at the traditional feast which opened the oyster season at the beginning of September.

Makes 1 rectangular cake, 30 cm × 20 cm (12 in × 8 in), or 24 squares
Time Preparation 10 minutes, Baking 1½ hours
Oven Temperature Gas Mark 2/150°C/300°F

Ingredients
250 g (8 oz) butter or hard margarine
250 g (8 oz) dark soft brown sugar
250 g (8 oz) black treacle
350 g (12 oz) plain flour
4 teaspoons ground ginger

3 teaspoons ground cinnamon
2 eggs, beaten
2 teaspoons bicarbonate of soda
300 ml (½ pint) lukewarm milk

Method
Put the fat, sugar and treacle into a pan and heat gently until the fat has melted. Sift the flour and spices into a bowl and pour in the treacle mixture. Add the eggs and beat until evenly coloured.

Stir the bicarbonate of soda into the lukewarm milk, pour into the cake mixture, and beat well. Grease and line a 30 cm × 20 cm (12 in × 8 in) cake tin. Pour in the gingerbread mixture, and bake for 1½ hours. Leave to stand in the tin for 5 minutes before cooling on a rack.

Sherry Almond Cake

This plain but delicious cake with a moist texture is excellent with tea, or with a glass of sherry in the Victorian style.

Makes 1 × 20 cm (8 in) cake
Time Preparation 15 minutes, Baking 1½ hours
Oven Temperature Gas Mark 4/180°C/350°F

Ingredients
250 g (8 oz) plain flour
1 teaspoon baking powder
pinch of salt
25 g (1 oz) ground rice
25 g (1 oz) ground almonds

250 g (8 oz) unsalted butter
250 g (8 oz) caster sugar
4 eggs, beaten
4 tablespoons dry sherry
few drops of almond essence

Method
Sieve the flour, baking powder and salt together, and stir in the rice and almonds until evenly mixed. Cream the butter and sugar until light and fluffy. Work in the flour and eggs alternately, beating well between additions, and stir in the sherry and essence.

Grease and lightly flour a 20 cm (8 in) round cake tin. Put in the mixture and bake for 1½ hours. Leave to cool in the tin for 5 minutes and then on a wire rack.

Seed Cake

Caraway used to be taken to aid the digestion, and this Victorian cake was popular as a contrast to the heavier fruit cake of the period.

Makes 1 × 17.5 cm (7 in) cake
Time Preparation 15 minutes, Baking 1¼ hours
Oven Temperature Gas Mark 4/180°C/350°F

Ingredients
250 g (8 oz) self-raising flour
pinch of ground nutmeg
1 teaspoon caraway seeds
250 g (8 oz) butter
250 g (8 oz) caster sugar

5 eggs, separated
75 g (3 oz) candied orange peel, chopped
2 tablespoons brandy

Topping
2 teaspoons caster sugar
½ teaspoon caraway seeds

3 teaspoons icing sugar, sieved

Method
Sieve the flour and nutmeg together and stir in the caraway seeds. Cream the butter and sugar until light and fluffy. Add the egg yolks, one at a time, to the creamed mixture, alternating with a teaspoon of the flour each time. Add the candied peel and fold in the remaining flour.

Whisk the egg whites until they form soft peaks and fold into the cake mixture. Stir in the brandy. Grease and base-line a 17.5 cm (7 in) round cake tin, and put the cake mixture into it.

Mix the caster sugar and caraway seeds and sprinkle on the cake. Bake for 1¼ hours. Cool in the tin for 10 minutes before turning on to a wire rack. When the cake is cold, sprinkle it with icing sugar.

98 *Top left* Colchester Gingerbread
(p. 97); *Top right* Orange Walnut
Cake (p. 97); *Bottom left* Country
Wholemeal Cake (p. 101); *Bottom
right* Seed Cake (p. 97)

Dundee Cake

This light citrus-flavoured cake, packed full of dried fruit, is distinguished by the pattern of browned almonds on top.

Makes 1 × 25 cm (10 in) cake
Time Preparation 20 minutes, Baking 2½ hours
Oven Temperature Gas Mark 3/160°C/325°F

Ingredients

250 g (8 oz) butter
250 g (8 oz) caster sugar
5 eggs, beaten
250 g (8 oz) self-raising flour
½ teaspoon ground nutmeg
grated rind of 1 lemon
grated rind of 1 orange
175 g (6 oz) currants
175 g (6 oz) sultanas
75 g (3 oz) glacé cherries, halved
50 g (2 oz) mixed candied peel, chopped
75 g (3 oz) ground almonds
50 g (2 oz) whole blanched almonds

Method

Cream the butter and sugar together until light and fluffy. Sieve the flour. Add the eggs and flour alternately to the creamed mixture, beating well after each addition. Fold in any remaining flour with the nutmeg and grated fruit rinds. Stir in the currants, sultanas, cherries and candied peel, and finally the ground almonds.

Grease and line a 25 cm (10 in) round cake tin. Put in the cake mixture and slightly hollow the surface with the base of a tablespoon. Bake for 1½ hours. Gently draw the cake part-way from the oven. Quickly arrange the almonds in circles on the top, putting them on very lightly, and return the cake to the oven and continue baking for 1 hour. Leave to cool in the tin for 10 minutes, then on a wire rack.

Arrange almonds on the Dundee Cake while it is half out of the oven.

Top Dundee Cake; *Bottom* Coconut Cake

Coconut Cake

A plain cake flavoured with coconut and orange is a delicious teatime treat. The surface is sprinkled with a mixture of coconut and icing sugar for an attractive appearance.

Makes 1 × 17.5 cm (7 in) cake
Time Preparation 15 minutes, Baking 1½ hours
Oven Temperature Gas Mark 4/180°C/350°F

Ingredients

300 g (10 oz) plain flour
1 teaspoon baking powder
pinch of salt
50 g (2 oz) desiccated coconut
grated rind and juice of 1 orange
150 g (5 oz) butter
175 g (6 oz) caster sugar
2 eggs, beaten
desiccated coconut and icing sugar, for sprinkling

Method

Sieve the flour with the baking powder and salt, and stir in the coconut and orange rind. Cream the butter and sugar until light and fluffy, and work in the flour and eggs alternately, beating well between each addition. Beat the orange juice into the mixture.

Grease and base-line a 17.5 cm (7 in) round cake tin and put in the cake mixture. Bake for 1½ hours. Cool in the tin for 5 minutes and then on a wire rack. Sprinkle the surface with a little coconut and icing sugar when cold.

Wholefood Cakes

MANY OF OUR traditional cakes could truly be described as 'wholefood' because the recipes date from the days when flour was brown and coarse, sugar was unrefined and oats and bran were store-cupboard standbys in country households. Commercial food firms developed techniques for refining foods during the nineteenth century, and white flour and white sugar were eagerly bought by people who thought them more acceptable and genteel than the rougher foods which their ancestors were forced to eat.

Today, the pendulum of fashion has swung back, encouraged by nutritionists and by our own desire for healthy living. Essential roughage is now more trendily known as 'fibre', and this is remarkably easy to incorporate into tasty and nutritious cakes and bakes.

These baked goods need not be heavy and unpalatable: today's ingredients can remain pure and good, with modern processing ensuring that they are clean and easy to use. Wholemeal flour can be light enough to make a sponge sandwich or be full of the delicious bits and pieces which give texture to fruit cakes and gingerbreads. Eggs may be free-range and richly flavoured, while fats may be made from vegetable oils. Extra fibre can be given by the use of grains such as oats, or by incorporating muesli mixture, while nuts and dried fruit add both fibre and sweetness. Unrefined natural sugars give both flavour and colour, while honey and black treacle add their own unique flavours.

Nutty Loaf

The yoghurt and oil in this cake make it very light. It may be eaten plain or spread with butter or honey.

Makes 1 × 750 g (1½ lb) loaf
Time Preparation 10 minutes, Baking 1¼ hours
Oven Temperature Gas Mark 5/190°C/375°F

Ingredients
175 g (6 oz) self-raising wholemeal flour
25 g (1 oz) bran
1 teaspoon bicarbonate of soda
½ teaspoon ground mixed spice
pinch of salt
125 g (4 oz) dark soft brown sugar
125 g (4 oz) chopped walnuts or hazelnuts
150 ml (¼ pint) natural yoghurt
4 tablespoons vegetable oil
1 egg, beaten
2 teaspoons grated orange rind

Method
Put the flour, bran, bicarbonate of soda, spice, salt, sugar and nuts into a bowl and stir until evenly coloured. Mix together the yoghurt, oil, egg and orange rind and beat into the dry ingredients.

Grease and base-line a 750 g (1½ lb) loaf tin. Put in the cake mixture and bake for 1¼ hours. Cool in the tin for 10 minutes and then on a wire rack.

Country Wholemeal Cake

The fat saved from a weekend joint makes a richly flavoured addition to a wholemeal cake which is very cheap to make.

Makes 1 × 15 cm (6 in) cake
Time Preparation 45 minutes, Baking 1¼ hours
Oven Temperature Gas Mark 4/180°C/350°F

Ingredients
250 g (8 oz) mixed dried fruit and peel
75 g (3 oz) clarified beef dripping*
150 g (5 oz) light soft brown sugar
250 ml (8 fl oz) water
250 g (8 oz) plain wholemeal flour
1 teaspoon baking powder
½ teaspoon bicarbonate of soda
pinch of ground nutmeg
pinch of ground cinnamon
pinch of ground mixed spice

* Warm the beef dripping until it is just liquid and pour it into a bowl containing 300 ml (½ pint) boiling water. Stir well for 4 minutes and then leave to get cold. Impurities will sink to the bottom and the solid dripping will be pure and smooth and suitable for use in cakes or pastry.

Method
Put the fruit, dripping, sugar and water into a thick saucepan. Bring to the boil, then reduce the heat and simmer for 10 minutes. Cool for 30 minutes.

Sieve together the flour, baking powder, bicarbonate of soda and spices, and blend into the fruit mixture until well mixed. Do not beat.

Grease and base-line a 15 cm (6 in) round cake tin. Put in the cake mixture, and bake for 1¼ hours. Cool in the tin for 5 minutes before turning on to a wire rack to cool completely.

Carrot Cake

Carrots give sweetness to this simple cake which is flavoured with almonds and lemon.

Makes 1 × 17.5 cm (7 in) cake
Time Preparation 15 minutes, Baking 1½ hours
Oven Temperature Gas Mark 4/180°C/350°F

Ingredients

250 g (8 oz) soft margarine	125 g (4 oz) ground almonds
250 g (8 oz) light soft brown sugar	4 eggs, beaten
250 g (8 oz) plain wholemeal flour	250 g (8 oz) carrots, grated
	grated rind and juice of 1 lemon

Topping

50 g (2 oz) chopped mixed nuts	25 g (1 oz) demerara sugar

Method

Put the margarine, sugar, flour, ground almonds and eggs into a bowl. Beat very hard until the mixture is light and fluffy, then beat in the carrots and the lemon rind and juice.

Grease and base-line a 17.5 cm (7 in) round cake tin. Put in the cake mixture and bake for 1 hour. Mix the nuts and demerara sugar together. Gently draw out the oven shelf so that the cake comes half-way out of the oven, sprinkle on the nut mixture and continue baking for 30 minutes. Cool in the tin for 10 minutes, then on a wire rack.

Banana and Cherry Loaf

This light teabread is flavoured with cherries and sultanas, and may be spread with butter or left plain.

Makes 1 × 1 kg (2 lb) loaf
Time Preparation 10 minutes, Baking 1½ hours
Oven Temperature Gas Mark 3/160°C/325°F

Ingredients

125 g (4 oz) soft margarine	2 eggs, beaten
175 g (6 oz) light soft brown sugar	125 g (4 oz) sultanas
250 g (8 oz) self-raising wholemeal flour	50 g (2 oz) glacé cherries, chopped
4 medium bananas, mashed	25 g (1 oz) chopped walnuts

Method

Cream the margarine and sugar until soft and fluffy. Work in the flour, bananas and eggs, and beat well. Fold in the sultanas, cherries and walnuts.

Grease and base-line a 1 kg (2 lb) loaf tin. Put in the cake mixture and bake for 1½ hours. Cool in the tin for 10 minutes, then on a wire rack.

Honey Loaf

This honey-flavoured cake may be eaten plain or spread with butter. If dates are not liked, mixed dried fruit may be used.

Makes 1 × 1 kg (2 lb) loaf
Time Preparation 15 minutes, Baking 1¼ hours
Oven Temperature Gas Mark 4/180°C/350°F

Ingredients

125 g (4 oz) clear honey	2 teaspoons baking powder
50 g (2 oz) light soft brown sugar	1 teaspoon salt
1 egg	½ teaspoon bicarbonate of soda
15 g (½ oz) melted butter	175 g (6 oz) chopped dates
125 g (4 oz) bran cereal	50 g (2 oz) chopped walnuts
300 g (10 oz) plain wholemeal flour	350 ml (12 fl oz) milk

Method

Put the honey, sugar, egg and butter into a bowl and beat well until evenly mixed. Stir in the bran cereal. Mix the flour with the baking powder, salt and bicarbonate of soda until evenly coloured. Add the dates and nuts. Add the flour mixture alternately with the milk to the honey mixture, stirring well but not beating.

Grease and base-line a 1 kg (2 lb) loaf tin. Put in the cake mixture and bake for 1¼ hours. Cool in the tin for 10 minutes and then on a wire rack.

Top Wholemeal Sponge Sandwich;
Bottom Banana Bars

Wholemeal Sponge Sandwich

This version of the popular Victoria Sandwich has a golden-brown colour and good flavour. The secret of success lies in beating the ingredients very hard until they are light and soft, and the best result is achieved with a food processor.

Makes 1 × 17.5 cm (7 in) cake
Time Preparation 15 minutes, Baking 30 minutes
Oven Temperature Gas Mark 4/180°C/350°F

Ingredients
175 g (6 oz) soft margarine
175 g (6 oz) light soft brown sugar
3 eggs, beaten

175 g (6 oz) self-raising wholemeal flour
1 teaspoon baking powder

Filling
125 g (4 oz) low-sugar apricot or raspberry jam

caster sugar, for sprinkling

Method
Cream the butter and sugar together until very light and fluffy. Sieve the flour and baking powder together. Add to the creamed mixture alternately with the eggs and beat well until thoroughly mixed. Put into two greased and base-lined 17.5 cm (7 in) sponge sandwich tins, and bake for 30 minutes. Turn on to a wire rack to cool.

Sandwich the cakes together with jam, and sprinkle the surface lightly with caster sugar.

Food Processor Method
Put all the ingredients into a food processor and process until very light and creamy.

Banana Bars

This cake may be left plain but it becomes very special when finished with a light cream cheese topping.

Makes 1 rectangular cake, 27.5 cm × 17.5 cm (11 in × 7 in), *or* 15 bars
Time Preparation 20 minutes, Baking 30 minutes
Oven Temperature Gas Mark 4/180°C/350°F

Ingredients
175 g (6 oz) plain wholemeal flour
50 g (2 oz) bran
1½ teaspoons baking powder
¼ teaspoon ground allspice
¼ teaspoon salt

2 eggs
175 g (6 oz) light soft brown sugar
9 tablespoons salad oil
½ teaspoon vanilla essence
3 medium bananas, mashed
75 g (3 oz) chopped walnuts

Icing
75 g (3 oz) full fat soft cream cheese
50 g (2 oz) butter or soft margarine

½ teaspoon vanilla or lemon essence
350 g (12 oz) icing sugar

Method
Stir together the flour, bran, baking powder, allspice and salt. Beat together the eggs, sugar, oil and essence, and add the mashed bananas. Work into the dry ingredients and beat well. Stir in the nuts.

Grease a 27.5 cm × 17.5 cm (11 in × 7 in) deep tin and put in the mixture. Bake for 30 minutes. Cool in the tin for 10 minutes, then on a wire rack.

Cream together the cream cheese and the butter or margarine until very light. Add the essence and beat in the sugar until soft and fluffy. Spread over the cake, and cut into bars before serving.

Perfect Sponge Cakes

ASPONGE IS MADE without fat; a sponge sandwich includes fat. (The cake known as Genoese sponge is a hybrid, needing a little melted fat to improve its flavour and keeping quality.) A sponge stales more quickly than a sandwich, and should be eaten within a couple of days, while a sandwich cake will keep for a week.

Both types of sponge cake should rise evenly with level, not domed, tops. The texture must be even, and neither too close nor too open. A sponge will rise without using a raising agent, as rising depends on the amount of air beaten into the mixture, but self-raising flour or baking powder are used in some recipes to be quite certain of a good 'rise'. Air must always be kept in the batter, and the flour should be sieved to incorporate air, and then folded in gently. The texture of sponge mixture should be a light whipped cream, but it is important not to over-beat with an electric mixer, or the cake will become flat when baked.

A food processor produces very good sandwich cakes and is quick to use if soft margarine is one of the ingredients. When using a processor, all the ingredients may be placed in the bowl at the same time, but an additional 1½ teaspoons of baking powder should be added to a three-egg cake to replace the air which is lost when a mixture is beaten in a closed bowl. Extra air may be incorporated if the small closing funnel is left out of the lid during beating.

Caster sugar is an important ingredient for successful sponge cakes, as it dissolves easily into the eggs in a whisked mixture, and creams easily with fat in a sandwich. The traditional egg weight for sandwich cakes is 50 g (2 oz) and size 3 eggs are the best to use. If the eggs are much larger or smaller, or are of very variable size, they should be weighed. The amount of sugar, fat and flour should be double the eggs' weight, so recipes may be adjusted easily.

Sponge cake mixtures are very delicate, and tins must be prepared carefully to prevent sticking. They should be brushed with melted butter and dusted with flour for a whisked sponge. For sandwich cakes, the tins should be greased and base-lined with greaseproof paper or baking parchment. For sponge cakes which require a crusty exterior (e.g. Sponge Drops), a little caster sugar is also sprinkled on the tin with the flour. When cakes are removed from the oven, it is best to leave them in the tin for a minute or two to firm up. For a perfect appearance, turn the cake quickly on to a hand and place base downwards on a wire rack to cool completely. If the cake is turned with the surface down on the rack, the light cake begins to sink slightly through the wire mesh, causing an unsightly marking. While this may not matter for family use, marks would be lost for this fault in competitions.

Flavourings

Sponges and sandwiches are traditionally flavoured with vanilla, but other essences may be used. *Lemon* or *orange* flavour may be added with grated rind and juice. *Chocolate* flavour is added by substituting a tablespoon or two of cocoa for the equivalent flour. *Coffee* may be added with essence, or with instant coffee powder or granules dissolved in a little hot water. These flavourings may also be introduced into the fillings and icings which accompany the cake mixture.

Victoria Sponge Sandwich

This is an adaptable recipe which may be flavoured with coffee, orange, lemon or chocolate and filled with appropriate butter icing, or may be left plain and filled with jam or lemon curd.

Makes 1 × 17.5 cm (7 in) cake
Time Preparation 10 minutes, Baking 30 minutes
Oven Temperature Gas Mark 4/180°C/350°F

Ingredients

175 g (6 oz) butter or soft margarine
175 g (6 oz) caster sugar
3 eggs, beaten

175 g (6 oz) self-raising flour
jam or lemon curd
caster sugar, for sprinkling

Method

The fat for this recipe should be at room temperature. Cream together the fat and sugar until very light and fluffy. Add the eggs, a little at a time, to the creamed mixture, beating well after each addition.

Put the flour into a sieve and gently sieve it by shaking over the creamed mixture until about one-quarter of the flour has been sieved. Fold this lightly into the creamed mixture with a metal spoon. Repeat the process until all the flour has been added.

Grease and base-line two 17.5 cm (7 in) sponge sandwich tins. Divide the mixture between them, and bake for 30 minutes. Leave in the tins for 1 minute and turn on to a wire rack to cool. Sandwich the two halves together with jam or lemon curd and sprinkle the top with caster sugar.

Food Processor Method

Use soft margarine and add 1½ teaspoons baking powder. Put all the ingredients into the food processor, and process until very light and creamy. Bake as for the traditional method above.

Sponge Drops

These little cakes are delicious with a filling of jam and cream, but butter icing may be used instead.

Makes 10–12 small cakes
Time Preparation 15 minutes, Baking 7–10 minutes
Oven Temperature Gas Mark 6/200°C/400°F

Ingredients

2 eggs, separated
pinch of salt
75 g (3 oz) caster sugar

75 g (3 oz) plain flour
¼ teaspoon baking powder
caster sugar, for sprinkling

Filling and Topping
4 tablespoons jam
150 ml (¼ pint) whipping cream

icing sugar, for sprinkling

Method

Put the egg whites into a bowl with the salt, and whisk to stiff peaks. Gradually whisk in the sugar and egg yolks alternately until the mixture is thick and creamy. Sieve the flour and baking powder together, and fold into the egg mixture.

Grease and flour two baking sheets. Put dessertspoonfuls of the mixture on the sheets, allowing a little room for spreading. Sprinkle lightly with caster sugar.

Bake for 7–10 minutes, and then cool on a wire rack.

Spread the flat side of half the cakes with jam. Whip the cream and use it to sandwich the cakes together. Sprinkle with icing sugar.

Whisked Sponge

This very light sponge cake is made without fat and is best eaten when freshly baked. The cake should be put together with jam or lemon curd; it is too light to pair with butter icing.

Makes 1 × 17.5 cm (7 in) cake
Time Preparation 10 minutes, Baking 25 minutes
Oven Temperature Gas Mark 4/180°C/350°F

Ingredients

3 eggs, separated
75 g (3 oz) caster sugar
75 g (3 oz) plain flour
½ teaspoon baking powder
jam or lemon curd
caster sugar, for sprinkling

Method

Put the egg yolks and sugar into a bowl, and whisk until very light and fluffy and almost white. Sieve the flour and baking powder together. Whisk the egg whites until they form stiff peaks. Fold the flour and egg whites alternately into the egg yolks.

Grease and base-line two 17.5 cm (7 in) sponge tins. Put in the mixture, and bake for 25 minutes. Leave in the tins for 2 minutes, then turn on to a wire rack to cool. Put the two halves together with jam or lemon curd and sprinkle with caster sugar.

Swiss Roll

A little care is needed to make the perfect Swiss Roll, but the results are very worth while.

Makes 1 swiss roll
Time Preparation 10 minutes, Baking 10 minutes
Oven Temperature Gas Mark 6/200°C/400°F

Ingredients

3 eggs
140 g (4½ oz) caster sugar
75 g (3 oz) plain flour
½ teaspoon baking powder
1 tablespoon cold water
6 tablespoons jam or lemon
  curd
caster sugar, for sprinkling

Method

Whisk the eggs and sugar together until very light and fluffy and almost white. Sift the flour and baking powder together and fold into the egg mixture with the water.

Grease and line a swiss roll tin. Lightly spread the mixture to cover the base of the tin, and bake for 10 minutes *exactly*.

While the cake is cooking, put a large piece of greaseproof paper on a flat surface and sprinkle with a little caster sugar. Turn the hot, cooked cake on to this sugared paper. With a sharp knife, quickly trim the edges of the cake to cut off the hard edges.

Have the jam just warm enough to spread easily. Spread it quickly on the cake and roll up firmly from a short end. Cover with a clean cloth while the cake cools, to keep it soft. Just before serving, sprinkle with caster sugar.

Top Geranium Sponge; *Bottom* Swiss Roll

Geranium Sponge

This is an old-fashioned sponge cake which is not filled. It has a lightly scented flavour, and is very good at teatime, or served with a dish of soft fruit. The type of geranium to use is the old-fashioned pot plant variety with feathery leaves and a strong scent such as rose, lemon or orange.

Makes 1 × 20 cm (8 in) cake
Time Preparation 15 minutes, Baking 45 minutes
Oven Temperature Gas Mark 3/160°C/325°F

Ingredients

4 eggs
125 g (4 oz) caster sugar
125 g (4 oz) plain flour
25 g (1 oz) cornflour
grated rind of ½ lemon
4 rose geranium leaves
caster sugar, for sprinkling

Method

Put two whole eggs and two egg yolks into a bowl. Add the sugar, and beat together for about 10 minutes until the mixture is very thick and pale. Sieve the flour and cornflour together, and fold into the mixture with the lemon rind. Whisk the remaining egg whites until they form stiff peaks and fold them into the cake mixture.

Grease and base-line a 20 cm (8 in) round cake tin, and sprinkle lightly with a mixture of flour and caster sugar. Put the geranium leaves on the base of the tin. Pour in the cake mixture, and bake for 45 minutes until firm and golden. Turn on to a wire rack to cool, and remove the leaves. Sprinkle the top with caster sugar.

Genoese Sponge

This light but firm-textured sponge with a delicious flavour of butter may be made as a simple cake, or it may be baked in a square tin and cut into shapes to be finished with icing. It is a good cake for shaping into novelty birthday cakes.

Makes 1 × 20 cm (8 in) cake
Time Preparation 15 minutes, Baking 30 minutes
Oven Temperature Gas Mark 5/190°C/375°F

Ingredients

4 eggs	75 g (3 oz) melted butter,
125 g (4 oz) caster sugar	cooled
75 g (3 oz) plain flour	caster sugar, for sprinkling

Method

Put the eggs and sugar into a bowl and place over a pan of hot but not boiling water, making sure that the bowl does not touch the surface of the water. Whisk until the mixture is light and thick. Sieve the flour.

Remove the bowl from the heat and continue whisking for 3 minutes. Fold in half the flour and the butter very gently. Fold in the remaining flour, stirring as little as possible.

Grease and flour a 30 cm (8 in) sponge sandwich tin. Pour in the cake mixture, and bake for 30 minutes. Cool on a wire rack. When cool, the cake may be sprinkled with sugar or finished with icing, and cut into shapes if liked.

Whisk eggs and sugar in a bowl over a pan of hot water.

Chocolate Cakes

A CHOCOLATE CAKE IS always very popular, whether it is a light, feathery sponge or a richer, moister mixture which is very dark and full of flavour. Chocolate cakes are usually made by the creamed method, but the flavour may be introduced in a variety of ways.

Cocoa is the most commonly used flavouring in chocolate cakes, giving a pure rich flavour. The cocoa powder may simply be added to the flour and other dry ingredients, but the flavour is enhanced if the powder is warmed through in water or milk from the recipe to make a chocolate paste: the cells burst and release their full flavour into the cake mixture before it is baked.

Drinking chocolate powder contains milk and sugar and has a lighter, sweeter flavour than cocoa, and it gives a slightly paler colour to the finished cake. If drinking chocolate is used as a substitute for cocoa in a recipe, the sugar content of the cake should be lessened slightly.

Block chocolate may be used for both cake and icing. The chocolate should be melted in a bowl over hot water (or in a microwave oven), and should then be added to the cake mixture when it is cool but still liquid. Plain chocolate has a better flavour than milk chocolate for baking, and the dark colour gives a richer appearance. Chocolate-flavoured blocks which are sold for cake- and confectionery-making are easy to use, as they melt easily and quickly and spread evenly, but some people find the texture fatty and do not enjoy the flavour.

Complementary Flavourings

While chocolate is delicious on its own, its flavour may be enhanced by a wide range of other flavourings. Vanilla essence is the traditional enhancer of chocolate, serving to bring out flavour and adding only a light perfume of its own. Coffee is another popular additive, and only a pinch of coffee powder or a few drops of coffee essence added to chocolate produce the sophisticated *mocha* flavour. Cinnamon and ginger are unusual but good too.

For special occasions, spirits and liqueurs blend well with chocolate if introduced into an icing or soaking syrup. Rum, brandy, whisky and orange-flavoured liqueurs are particularly useful to blend beautifully with plain chocolate. Orange rind and juice introduce a fresh flavour, while bananas give a moistness and rich flavour to chocolate cakes. Pears and chocolate are natural partners and pears are very good in the filling of a chocolate cake. If butter icing is considered too rich for a cake filling, raspberry or apricot jam is plainer and goes beautifully with such a cake.

Dark Chocolate Cake

The best kind of chocolate cake is rich and dark, and this one is very quick to make.

Makes 1 × 17.5 cm (7 in) cake
Time Preparation 15 minutes, Baking 30 minutes
Oven Temperature Gas Mark 4/180°C/350°F

Ingredients

125 g (4 oz) soft margarine
175 g (6 oz) dark soft brown sugar
2 eggs, beaten
175 g (6 oz) plain flour

Icing and Decoration
125 g (4 oz) plain chocolate, broken into pieces
1 tablespoon milk

1 teaspoon baking powder
½ teaspoon bicarbonate of soda
150 ml (¼ pint) Guinness
50 g (2 oz) cocoa

125 g (4 oz) soft margarine
250 g (8 oz) icing sugar
12 walnut halves

Method

Cream the margarine and sugar together until light and fluffy. Sieve together the flour, baking powder and bicarbonate of soda, and work into the creamed mixture alternately with the eggs, beating well between each addition. Mix the Guinness and cocoa to a paste, and stir into the cake mixture until evenly coloured.

Grease and base-line two 17.5 cm (7 in) sponge tins. Pour in the mixture, and bake for 30 minutes. Turn on to a wire rack to cool.

To make the icing, put the chocolate and milk into a bowl over hot water. Heat until the chocolate has melted, and then leave until lukewarm. Beat together the fat and sugar until light and fluffy, then gradually beat in the chocolate until the icing is evenly coloured. Spread one-third of the icing on the flat side of one cake, put the other cake on top and spread the surface with the remaining icing. Decorate with walnut halves.

Milk Chocolate Cake

Although plain chocolate and cocoa are preferable to give depth of flavour to chocolate cakes, some people like the lightness and sweetness of milk chocolate and will appreciate this cake.

Makes 1 × 20 cm (8 in) cake
Time Preparation 15 minutes, Baking 25–30 minutes
Oven Temperature Gas Mark 4/180°C/350°F

Ingredients

125 g (4 oz) soft margarine
125 g (4 oz) caster sugar
3 eggs
150 g (5 oz) self-raising flour

125 g (4 oz) drinking chocolate powder
1 teaspoon baking powder

Filling and Icing
4 tablespoons apricot jam
175 g (6 oz) milk chocolate, broken into pieces

15 g (½ oz) butter

Method

Put the margarine, sugar and eggs into a bowl. Sieve the flour, chocolate powder and baking powder together and add to the other ingredients. Beat the mixture very hard until it is light and creamy.

Grease and base-line two 20 cm (8 in) sponge tins. Put in the cake mixture, and bake for 25–30 minutes. Cool on a wire rack.

Sandwich the cakes together with apricot jam. Put the chocolate and butter into a bowl over hot water and heat gently until the chocolate has melted. Beat well and pour over the cake.

Top Chocolate Marble Cake; *Bottom* Milk Chocolate Cake

Chocolate Marble Cake

Plain and chocolate mixtures mingle in this attractive cake. The plain cake may be tinted with pink colouring if liked.

Makes 1 × 20 cm (8 in) cake
Time Preparation 15 minutes, Baking 45–55 minutes
Oven Temperature Gas Mark 4/180°C/350°F

Ingredients

175 g (6 oz) soft margarine
175 g (6 oz) caster sugar
175 g (6 oz) self-raising flour
1½ teaspoons baking powder

3 eggs, beaten
1 tablespoon cocoa
1 tablespoon hot water
icing sugar, for sprinkling

Method

Put the fat and sugar into a bowl and cream until light and fluffy. Sieve the flour and baking powder together and add to the creamed mixture alternately with the eggs, beating well between each addition. Mix the cocoa and water in a bowl and add one-third of the cake mixture, beating well until evenly coloured.

Grease and base-line a 20 cm (8 in) round cake tin. Put spoonfuls of the plain mixture over the base at intervals, leaving gaps. Spoon chocolate mixture into the gaps and top with more spoonfuls of plain mixture. Do not smooth out the mixture or try to mix the colours. Bake for 45–55 minutes. Turn on to a wire rack to cool. Sprinkle with icing sugar just before serving.

Chocolate Almond Cake

Almonds give a delicate flavour to this chocolate cake and are also used to decorate the rich chocolate icing.

Makes 1 × 20 cm (8 in) cake
Time Preparation 20 minutes, Baking 45 minutes
Oven Temperature Gas Mark 3/160°C/325°F

Ingredients
175 g (6 oz) soft margarine	3 eggs
175 g (6 oz) caster sugar	25 g (1 oz) ground almonds
175 g (6 oz) self-raising flour	few drops of almond essence
1½ teaspoons baking powder	

Icing and Decoration
75 g (3 oz) butter or hard margarine	50 g (2 oz) plain chocolate, broken into pieces
250 g (8 oz) light soft brown sugar	250 g (8 oz) icing sugar
3 tablespoons water	50 g (2 oz) flaked almonds
1 tablespoon instant coffee powder	

Method
Cream the fat and sugar until light and fluffy. Sieve the flour and baking powder together and add to the creamed mixture alternately with the eggs, beating well between each addition. Beat in the ground almonds and almond essence.

Grease and base-line two 20 cm (8 in) sponge tins. Put in the mixture, and bake for 45 minutes. Turn on to a wire rack to cool.

To make the icing, put the fat, sugar, water, coffee and chocolate into a pan, and heat gently until the chocolate and fat have melted. Stir well and then leave until lukewarm. Beat in the icing sugar to make a soft icing. Use one-third of the icing to sandwich the cakes together and spread the rest over the top of the cake. Sprinkle on the flaked almonds.

Mocha Cake

Chocolate and coffee complement each other wonderfully well, and this cake has a subtle flavour of both.

Makes 1 × 20 cm (8 in) cake
Time Preparation 10 minutes, Baking 1 hour
Oven Temperature Gas Mark 4/180°C/350°F

Ingredients
175 g (6 oz) butter	2 tablespoons coffee essence
175 g (6 oz) caster sugar	50 g (2 oz) plain chocolate, grated coarsely
175 g (6 oz) self-raising flour	icing sugar, for sprinkling
3 eggs, beaten	

Method
Cream the butter and sugar until light and fluffy. Sieve the flour and add to the creamed mixture alternately with the eggs, beating well between each addition. Fold in the coffee essence and grated chocolate.

Grease and line a 20 cm (8 in) round cake tin. Put in the cake mixture, and bake for 1 hour. Cool in the tin for 5 minutes and then on a wire rack. Sprinkle the surface with icing sugar just before serving.

Chocolate Rum Cake

Chocolate and rum are natural companions, and they blend together beautifully in this dark, rich cake.

Makes 1 × 17.5 cm (7 in) cake
Time Preparation 20 minutes, Baking 30 minutes
Oven Temperature Gas Mark 4/180°C/350°F

Ingredients
175 g (6 oz) butter	25 g (1 oz) cornflour
175 g (6 oz) caster sugar	25 g (1 oz) cocoa powder
6 tablespoons black treacle	4 tablespoons milk
2 eggs	1 tablespoon dark rum
175 g (6 oz) self-raising flour	

Filling, Icing and Decoration
250 g (8 oz) butter	2 tablespoons rum
350 g (12 oz) icing sugar	2 tablespoon boiling water
2 tablespoons black treacle	25 g (1 oz) plain chocolate, grated coarsely
6 tablespoons milk	

Method
Cream the butter, sugar and treacle until light and fluffy. Add the eggs one at a time, beating well after each addition. Sieve the flour, cornflour and cocoa together. Mix the milk and rum together. Fold the flour into the mixture alternately with the milk and rum.

Grease and base-line two 17.5 cm (7 in) round sandwich tins. Put in the cake mixture. Bake for 30 minutes and then turn on to a wire rack to cool. When the cakes are cold, split each one horizontally in half to make a total of four layers.

To make the icing, cream the butter, icing sugar and black treacle together until light and fluffy. Beat in the milk and rum very gradually. Add the boiling water a few drops at a time, beating well. Sandwich the layers of the cake together with this icing and cover the cake with the rest of the icing. Sprinkle with grated chocolate.

Small Cakes and Fast Bakes

INDIVIDUAL SMALL CAKES and squares or fingers cut from cakes baked in rectangular tins are extremely useful. They are quick and easy to make and portions may be conveniently controlled, which is a particular advantage if small children are being served. For guests, fresh pieces of cake can be produced, instead of a half-cut cake which is less inviting and appetising. Small cakes may be made in bun tins, or in paper cases which are easier to handle, particularly if they are being sold on a fund-raising stall.

Crunch Cake

This spiced cake with a crunchy topping is perfect to serve warm at a coffee party.

Makes 9 squares
Time Preparation 15 minutes, Baking 30 minutes
Oven Temperature Gas Mark 6/200°C/400°F

Ingredients
Topping
25 g (1 oz) plain flour	50 g (2 oz) demerara sugar
25 g (1 oz) fine semolina	40 g (1½ oz) chopped nuts
2 teaspoons ground cinnamon	40 g (1½ oz) melted butter, cooled

Cake
75 g (3 oz) plain flour	75 g (3 oz) caster sugar
75 g (3 oz) fine semolina	50 g (2 oz) butter, cut into pieces
pinch of salt	1 egg
3 teaspoons baking powder	6 tablespoons milk
1 teaspoons ground ginger	
1 teaspoon ground cinnamon	

icing sugar, for sprinkling

Method
The topping should be prepared before the cake mixture. Stir together the flour, semolina and cinnamon until evenly coloured. Stir in the sugar and nuts and mix with the butter. Leave until cool.

Sieve the flour and stir in the semolina, salt, baking powder, spices and sugar. Rub in the butter until the mixture is like fine breadcrumbs. Beat the egg and milk together, and beat into the mixture.

Grease and base-line a 17.5 cm (7 in) square tin. Put in the cake mixture, sprinkle with the topping, and bake for 30 minutes. Leave the cake in the tin for 10 minutes and then turn on to a wire rack. Serve warm with a little icing sugar sprinkled on top of the crunchy topping.

Top Crunch Cake; *Bottom* Raspberry Buns

Raspberry Buns

These old-fashioned little cakes have a sugared finish and a filling of raspberry jam.

Makes 15 cakes
Time Preparation 15 minutes, Baking 20 minutes
Oven Temperature Gas Mark 5/190°C/375°F

Ingredients
250 g (8 oz) plain flour	125 g (4 oz) caster sugar
2 teaspoons baking powder	6 tablespoons milk
pinch of salt	75 g (3 oz) raspberry jam
75 g (3 oz) butter or hard margarine, cut into pieces	caster sugar, for sprinkling

Method
Sieve the flour, baking powder and salt into a bowl. Rub in the butter or hard margarine until the mixture is like fine breadcrumbs. Stir in the sugar and mix to a firm dough with the milk.

Knead the dough on a lightly floured board until smooth. Roll out into 15 circles, about 10 cm (4 in) across. Put a spoonful of jam in the centre of each. Moisten the edges of the dough lightly and gather them to the centre to enclose the jam.

Grease and flour two baking sheets. Put on the cakes, smooth side uppermost. Make a small cross on the top of each with a knife, and bake for 15 minutes. Sprinkle lightly with caster sugar and continue baking for 5 minutes. Cool on a wire rack.

Lemon Crust Squares

The textures of this deliciously buttery cake and its lemon and sugar topping are a perfect contrast. Orange juice may be used instead of lemon, but the flavour is blander.

Makes 16 squares
Time Preparation 15 minutes, Baking 35 minutes
Oven Temperature Gas Mark 4/180°C/350°F

Ingredients

175 g (6 oz) butter	175 g (6 oz) self-raising flour
175 g (6 oz) caster sugar	2 eggs, beaten

Topping

125 g (4 oz) caster sugar	2 tablespoons lemon juice

Method
Cream the butter and sugar together until very light and fluffy. Sieve the flour and work it into the mixture alternately with the eggs to make a creamy batter.

Grease and line a 27.5 cm × 17.5 cm (11 in × 7 in) tin. Put in the cake mixture, and bake for 35 minutes. While the cake is baking, mix the sugar and lemon juice.

When the cake is cooked, do not turn it out of the tin. While the cake is warm, prick the top lightly with a fork, and quickly spread on the lemon mixture to cover the surface completely. Cool in the tin and cut into pieces when cold.

Butterscotch Brownies

These are very quickly made and are delicious on their own or with ice cream.

Makes 16 squares
Time Preparation 5 minutes, Baking 20 minutes
Oven Temperature Gas Mark 4/180°C/350°F

Ingredients

175 g (6 oz) dark soft brown sugar	½ teaspoon salt
75 g (3 oz) melted butter	½ teaspoon vanilla essence
1 egg, beaten	50 g (2 oz) chopped walnuts
150 g (5 oz) self-raising flour	icing sugar, for sprinkling

Method
Put the sugar into a bowl and stir in the butter until evenly mixed. Add the egg, flour, salt and vanilla essence. Beat well, then stir in the walnuts.

Grease a 20 cm (8 in) square tin and put in the mixture. Bake for 20 minutes, and then cool in the tin. Cut into squares, and sprinkle with icing sugar just before serving.

Melting Moments

These light little cakes are made with cornflour. They may be flavoured with a little coffee or cocoa if liked, but are very good plain with a simple cherry decoration.

Makes 18 cakes
Time Preparation 15 minutes, Baking 20 minutes
Oven Temperature Gas Mark 4/180°C/350°F

Ingredients

175 g (6 oz) unsalted butter	2 eggs, beaten
75 g (3 oz) caster sugar	few drops of vanilla essence
250 g (8 oz) cornflour	9 glacé cherries, halved
1 teaspoon baking powder	icing sugar, for sprinkling

Method
Cream the butter and sugar until very light and fluffy. Sieve the cornflour and baking powder together. Add the eggs and cornflour alternately to the creamed mixture, beating well between each addition. Flavour with vanilla essence.

Lightly grease 18 deep tart tins. Divide the mixture between the tins, and top each one with a cherry half. Bake for 20 minutes, then lift carefully on to a wire rack to cool. Sprinkle with icing sugar, and serve freshly baked.

Queen Cakes

If liked, the currants may be omitted, and then these light little cakes become 'fairy cakes'.

Makes 12 cakes
Time Preparation 10 minutes, Baking 12 minutes
Oven Temperature Gas Mark 5/190°C/375°F

Ingredients

50 g (2 oz) butter or soft margarine	1 egg, beaten
50 g (2 oz) caster sugar	1 tablespoon milk
50 g (2 oz) self-raising flour	few drops of vanilla essence
	50 g (2 oz) currants

Method
Cream the fat and sugar until light and fluffy. Sieve the flour and add to the creamed mixture alternately with the egg. Beat in the milk and vanilla essence and stir in the currants.

Place 12 paper cases in tart tins so that they remain in shape while baking. Divide the mixture between the paper cases, and bake for 12 minutes. Lift on to a wire rack to cool.

Gâteau St Honoré (p. 115)

*B*aking for
special occasions

*T*here are many occasions for which a special cake is required. During the year, there are birthdays, and family celebrations, as well as weddings, christenings and anniversaries. There are special teatimes at Easter and Christmas, numerous children's parties, and adults' parties when a gâteau can be served as an elegant dish for a buffet meal.

Although such cakes look spectacular, they are surprisingly easy to assemble from basic recipes. Sponge cake mixtures, pastry and choux pastry can be put together in many different ways and with a variety of icings to make special cakes which can look very professional indeed.

Meringues

Meringues keep well in an airtight container or the freezer, and can be filled quickly with cream or ice cream, and fruit if liked.

Makes 16 meringue shells
Time Preparation 10 minutes, Baking 1½ hours
Oven Temperature Gas Mark 1/140°C/275°F

Ingredients
3 egg whites   double cream, for filling
175 g (6 oz) caster sugar

Method
Put the egg whites into a very clean, dry bowl which is free from any grease. Whisk until they form stiff peaks. Add 25 g (1 oz) sugar and continue whisking until the sugar is incorporated. Add 25 g (1 oz) sugar and whisk again. Repeat once more and then fold in the remaining sugar.

Line two baking sheets with baking parchment. Use two dessertspoons to shape 16 meringues on the baking sheets. Bake for 1½ hours. Turn off the heat, but leave the meringues in the oven until cold. Store in an airtight container. To serve, whip the cream until it forms soft peaks and sandwich the meringues together in pairs.

Brandy Snaps

These crisp tubes of lacy biscuit are delicious just as they
are or filled with whipped cream.

Makes 12 brandy snaps
Time Preparation 10 minutes, Baking 10 minutes
Oven Temperature Gas Mark 4/180°C/350°F

Ingredients

50 g (2 oz) golden syrup	50 g (2 oz) plain flour
40 g (1½ oz) caster sugar	1 teaspoon ground ginger
50 g (2 oz) butter	1 teaspoon brandy

Method
Put the syrup, sugar and butter into a thick pan and heat
gently until the sugar has melted and the mixture is
smooth. Sieve the flour and ginger together. Take the
saucepan from the heat and stir in the flour mixture and the
brandy. Leave to cool to lukewarm.

Lightly grease two baking sheets. Take out
teaspoonfuls of the mixture and roll lightly into even-sized
balls with the hands. Put on to the baking sheets, allowing
7.5 cm (3 in) between them. Bake for 10 minutes, when the
biscuits will be very thin, lacy and golden-brown.

While the biscuits are baking, grease the handles of two
or three wooden spoons. Remove the biscuits from the oven
and leave them to stand for 2 minutes. Lift them off the
baking sheets carefully with a palette knife. Wrap at once
round the handle of a wooden spoon. Slip off and cool on a
rack. If the biscuits become brittle on the tin, put the
baking sheet back in the oven for a few seconds to soften
them again. Store in an airtight container. Serve unfilled or
with whipped cream piped in.

Christmas Tree Gâteau

Christmas Tree Gâteau

Small choux pastry balls filled with cream can be piled into a cone shape with the aid of caramel syrup, and then decorated to make a 'tree' for a Christmas party.

Makes 1 gâteau
Time Preparation 45 minutes, Baking 20 minutes
Oven Temperature Gas Mark 6/200°C/400°F

Ingredients

double recipe for choux pastry for Eclairs (p. 118)   450 ml (¾ pint) double cream

Caramel Syrup
175 g (6 oz) granulated sugar   pinch of cream of tartar
150 ml (¼ pint) water

Decorations
mixed coloured glacé cherries   small Christmas tree baubles (optional)
silver balls

Method
Prepare the choux pastry as for Eclairs (page 118). Pipe or spoon into small balls about the size of small walnuts on to baking sheets rinsed in cold water but not dried. Bake for 20 minutes. Lift on to a wire rack and make a small slit in the side of each ball to release the steam.

Whip the cream and fill the cold choux pastry balls. Make the syrup by dissolving the sugar slowly in the water, without stirring. Add the cream of tartar, and boil rapidly to a pale golden colour. Remove from the heat. Take a thick cake board and place it on a firm, flat surface.

Quickly dip the balls into the syrup, on one side, taking care not to burn your fingers, and arrange on the board to form a 20 cm (8 in) circle, letting the balls stick together. Fill in the centre of the circle in the same way. Form a second layer slightly smaller and continue in tapering layers to form a cone.

Make sure that any remaining cream is stiff enough to pipe into rosettes. Pipe rosettes at intervals on the tree and decorate with halved coloured cherries or silver balls. If wished, place a Christmas bauble at the tip of the 'tree' and other baubles at the base. Take a fork and pull threads from the caramel to wrap around the tree. (If the syrup becomes too set, warm it slightly to soften.) Serve freshly made.

Christmas Log Cake

This is a traditional Christmas cake in France, and many families in this country like it as an alternative to the usual fruit cake. If liked, butter icing may be used as the filling instead of chestnut purée.

Makes 1 log
Time Preparation 20 minutes (plus cake-baking time)

Ingredients
1 Swiss Roll (p. 105)

Filling
125 g (4 oz) chestnut purée or vanilla Butter Icing (p. 121)

Icing
65 g (2½ oz) unsalted butter   50 g (2 oz) plain chocolate
50 g (2 oz) caster sugar   icing sugar, sieved, for
1 egg yolk   decoration
2 tablespoons rum, Grand Marnier or milk

Method
Prepare and bake the Swiss Roll, filling it with chestnut purée (from a tube or can) or vanilla butter icing. Place on a serving board or plate.

Cream the butter, sugar and egg yolk and work in the rum, Grand Marnier or milk. Melt the chocolate in a bowl over hot water or in a microwave oven, and work into the chocolate mixture. Leave until cold, then spread over the Swiss Roll. With a fork, mark wavy lines in the chocolate to resemble the bark of a log. Leave until the chocolate is firm, and dust lightly with sieved icing sugar. Holly leaves and a robin may also be used for decoration if liked.

Roll up the filled sponge to form the log.

Pipe choux buns around the edge of the pastry ring for Gâteau St Honoré.

Gâteau St Honoré

This French favourite looks very impressive, but it is not difficult to assemble.

Makes 1 gâteau
Time Preparation 20 minutes, Baking 30 minutes
Oven Temperature Gas Mark 6/200°C/400°F

Ingredients

175 g (6 oz) made sweet
  shortcrust pastry (p. 67)
one recipe for choux pastry
  for Eclairs (p. 118)
300 ml (½ pint) double
  cream

75 g (3 oz) caster sugar
crystallised violets and rose
  petals, to decorate

Method

Roll out the pastry into a 20 cm (8 in) round. Grease a baking sheet and put the pastry on it. Prick well with a fork. Prepare the Eclair choux pastry mixture (page 118) and pipe 12–14 'buns' round the edge of the pastry circle on the top of the pastry, so that the 'buns' just touch. Pipe the remaining mixture on to a separate baking sheet rinsed in cold water but not dried, making 'buns' the same size as those on top of the pastry.

Bake for 30 minutes and cool the pastry circle and the 'buns' on a wire rack, slitting each one so that the steam escapes. Whip the cream until it forms soft peaks and fill all the 'buns'. Put the sugar into a small, heavy pan and heat it gently until golden and syrupy. Dip the bases of the 'buns' in this syrup, taking care not to burn your fingers, and stick them on top of the 'buns' on the pastry. Trickle any remaining syrup on top of the 'buns' and decorate at once with violets and rose petals. Pipe the remaining cream into the centre of the pastry base. Serve freshly made.

Fruit Gâteau

Genoese Sponge (page 106) or Victoria Sponge Sandwich (page 104) can be transformed into delicious gâteaux very quickly and easily. Pineapple and apricots are good fruits to use at any time of the year as the canned varieties are suitable. In the summer, fresh raspberries or strawberries may be used.

Makes 1 gâteau
Time Preparation 20 minutes (plus cake-baking time)

Ingredients

2 × 17.5 cm (7 in) sponge
  cakes
500 g (1 lb) canned pineapple
  or apricot halves or 500 g
  (1 lb) fresh raspberries or
  strawberries
2 tablespoons rum or kirsch

300 ml (½ pint) double
  cream
125 g (4 oz) flaked almonds
3 tablespoons apricot jam or
  redcurrant jelly
angelica and cherries, for
  decoration

Method

Split each of the sponge cakes in half so that they make four circles. Drain the canned fruit well if used. Reserve half the fruit and chop the rest roughly. (Raspberries may be left whole.) Sprinkle chopped pineapple with rum, or the other fruit with kirsch. Whip the cream until it forms soft peaks, and fold one-third of the cream into the fruit.

Put one piece of cake on a serving dish and sandwich together the layers with the fruit mixture. Whip the remaining cream until it forms firm peaks, and spread half of it round the sides of the cake. Spread the almonds on a baking sheet and toast under a medium grill until golden. Leave them to cool and then spread them on a piece of greaseproof paper. Gently lift the cake, holding it by the top and bottom, and roll it like a wheel on the almonds until the sides are coated. Place on the serving dish.

Spread a little of the cream over the cake, and arrange the fruit attractively on top. Heat the jam or jelly and brush it over the fruit to glaze it. Put the remaining cream into a piping bag and pipe stars around the edge of the gâteau and between the pieces of fruit. Decorate with small pieces of cherry and angelica, and serve freshly made.

Praline Cream Gâteau

This lovely cake, with its rather sophisticated flavour, is ideal for a buffet supper. The Praline (page 124) may be prepared a few days in advance.

Makes 1 × 25 cm (10 in) cake
Time Preparation 20 minutes, Baking 1¼ hours
Oven Temperature Gas Mark 4/180°C/350°F

Ingredients

250 g (8 oz) unsalted butter
250 g (8 oz) caster sugar
4 eggs
25 g (1 oz) ground almonds

300 g (10 oz) plain flour
2 teaspoons baking powder
2 tablespoons water

Praline Cream and Decoration
450 ml (¾ pint) double
  cream
125 g (4 oz) Praline (p. 124)

3 tablespoons apricot jam
75 g (3 oz) flaked almonds

Method

Cream the butter and sugar together until light and fluffy. Beat in the eggs one at a time, beating well between each addition. Stir in the ground almonds. Sieve the flour and baking powder together and fold into the mixture with the water. Put into a greased and base-lined 25 cm (10 in) round cake tin, and bake for 1¼ hours until firm. Cool on a wire rack.

To prepare the Praline Cream, whip the cream to stiff peaks and divide in half. Fold the praline into one half of the cream. Split the cake in half, and spread the base with apricot jam and two-thirds of the Praline Cream. Put the cake together. Spread half the plain cream round the edges of the cake.

Put the flaked almonds on to a baking sheet and toast under a medium grill until golden. Leave until cold and put on to a piece of greaseproof paper. Hold the cake like a wheel and coat the sides completely with the almonds. Spread the remaining plain cream on the top and decorate with whorls of the remaining Praline Cream and a few of the toasted almonds.

116 *Top left* Praline Cream Gâteau (p. 115); *Top right* Fruit Gâteau (p. 115); *Bottom left* Christmas Log Cake (p. 114); *Bottom right* Coffee Eclairs (p. 118)

Eclairs

Finger-lengths of choux pastry are delicious when filled with whipped cream and topped with coffee- or chocolate-flavoured icing. They should be filled and iced just before serving so that the cases remain crisp.

Makes 12 éclairs
Time Preparation 20 minutes, Baking 20 minutes
Oven Temperature Gas Mark 6/200°C/400°F, *then* Gas Mark 7/220°C/425°F

Ingredients

65 g (2½ oz) plain flour	pinch of salt
50 g (2 oz) butter	2 eggs
150 ml (¼ pint) water	

Filling and Icing

300 ml (½ pint) double cream	1 tablespoon boiling water
2 teaspoons instant coffee powder or cocoa	150 g (5 oz) icing sugar

Method

Sift the flour on to a piece of greaseproof paper. Put the butter and water into a pan and bring to the boil. As soon as the liquid boils, remove from the heat and shoot in all the flour at once, beating vigorously. Add the salt and beat until the mixture forms a ball, which will take about 1 minute.

Lightly beat the eggs in a separate bowl so that the whites and yolks are just mixed. Leave the dough to cool for 10 minutes. Using a wooden spoon (or food processor), beat in the eggs a little at a time, until the paste is smooth and glossy and stiff enough to stand in peaks.

Rinse a baking sheet in water, but do not dry it. Spoon or pipe the mixture into 7.5 cm (3 in) lengths on the baking sheet. Bake at the top of the oven for 10 minutes. Increase the oven heat and continue baking for 10 minutes.

Lift on to a wire rack, and immediately cut a 2.5 cm (1 in) slit in the side of each éclair with a sharp-pointed knife so that the steam escapes.

Do not fill the éclairs until about an hour before serving. Whip the cream until it forms soft peaks and spoon or pipe it into the éclair cases. Put the coffee powder or cocoa into a bowl and dissolve it in the boiling water. Work in the icing sugar until the mixture is like thick cream. Spread on the éclairs and leave to set.

Rich Fruit Cake

This cake will keep for up to a year if stored in an airtight tin. It is suitable for Christmas, birthdays or other celebrations, and for a wedding cake, when finished with Almond Paste and Royal Icing (pages 124 and 123).

Makes 1 × 25 cm (10 in) round *or* 22.5 cm (9 in) square cake
Time Preparation 30 minutes, Standing 1 hour, Baking 4½ hours
Oven Temperature Gas Mark 2/150°C/300°F

Ingredients

250 g (8 oz) butter	1 teaspoon ground mixed spice
250 g (8 oz) dark soft brown sugar	pinch of ground cinnamon
1 tablespoon black treacle	pinch of ground nutmeg
4 eggs	350 g (12 oz) currants
4 tablespoons brandy	350 g (12 oz) sultanas
grated rind of 1 lemon	250 g (8 oz) seedless raisins
½ teaspoon vanilla essence	50 g (2 oz) glacé cherries
175 g (6 oz) plain flour	50 g (2 oz) mixed candied peel, chopped
125 g (4 oz) self-raising flour	
¼ teaspoon salt	

Method

Grease and line a 25 cm (10 in) round or 22.5 cm (9 in) square tin with a double layer of greaseproof paper. Cream the butter and sugar until very light and fluffy. Beat together the treacle, eggs, brandy, lemon rind and vanilla essence in a bowl just enough to break up the eggs. Sieve the flours, salt and spices into a third bowl.

Add the egg mixture and flour alternately to the creamed mixture, stirring well but not beating. Add the fruit and candied peel, and mix just enough to distribute evenly. Put into the prepared tin and level the surface. Leave to stand for 1 hour and then bake for 4½ hours. Leave in the tin until lukewarm and then cool on a wire rack.

Larger Cake

For a 35 cm (14 in) round or 30 cm (12 in) square cake, double the quantities given in the recipe above and bake for about 7 hours, testing with a skewer to see if the cake is fully cooked.

Smaller Cake

For a 17.5 cm (7 in) round or 15 cm (6 in) square cake, halve the quantities given in the recipe above and bake for 2½–3 hours.

Rich Fruit Cake (p. 118) iced with
Simple Fondant Icing (p. 122) and
Royal Icing (p. 123) and decorated
with frosted violets

Icings, fillings and decoration

*S*imple icing is very attractive on home-baked cakes, and may be varied with different flavours and decorations. It is important to choose the correct icing for the type of cake. *Butter icing* is a mixture of butter (or soft margarine) with icing sugar which is suitable for filling and topping sponge sandwiches and gâteaux, and for sandwiching biscuits together. *Glacé icing* is made from icing sugar with water or fruit juice, which spreads easily and dries quickly, and it is suitable for small cakes, sponge sandwiches and biscuits. The icing cracks after a few days, so it should only be used on cakes which are to be eaten quickly. It will soften biscuits, and should be spread on them just before serving.

Fondant icing may be made with a sugar syrup, or by an uncooked method, and is very useful as it can be rolled out like pastry to coat sponge sandwiches, fruit cakes or gâteaux, and it is also suitable for moulding into flower shapes. This icing is usually placed over a coating of *almond paste*, made from ground almonds and sugar, which protects the icing from discoloration. This protection is also placed under *royal icing*, the firm mixture of egg whites and icing sugar traditional for wedding cakes and Christmas cakes. *American frosting*, too, is suitable for Christmas cakes, as well as for nut, spice and chocolate cakes, and is a fluffy boiled mixture of sugar syrup and egg whites with a crisp surface.

Icing Equipment

Simple icing does not require elaborate equipment, and it is best to buy the minimum necessary until your icing skills are perfected. *A nylon sieve* is essential for icing sugar, as a wire one may discolour the sugar. Only a *bowl and spoon* are needed for mixing, although an *electric whisk* is useful for one or two icings. A *turntable* aids the slow turning of a cake which is being iced so that the icing remains even and unsmudged, but a cake board on an upturned bowl is a useful substitute. A *palette knife* is also needed.

A *piping bag* is needed for piping edges and other decorations, and the 30 cm (12 in) size, made of either cloth or plastic, is the most useful. There is a huge range of piping nozzles, but a writing tube and large and small star nozzles will give plenty of patterns for the beginner.

Decorating a Cake

If both the top and sides of a cake are to be iced with *butter icing*, the sides should be coated first and then the cake may be rolled in chopped nuts, vermicelli or grated chocolate before the top is iced and decorated. Butter icing should always look soft and luscious, and may be finished simply by peaking the icing with a fork or wide spoon. It should not be pressed down heavily and spread flat, as this looks very unprofessional.

Before icing and decorating a cake, assemble any decorations, and take time to practise piping the type of edging or lettering required.

Piping

For piping, butter icing should be cool and firm. Glacé icing may be used for writing, but will need a little extra icing sugar to make it firm enough to pipe. Royal icing for edges and decorations such as rosettes must be stiff enough to stand in well-formed peaks, but for writing or trellises, the icing should be softer (or the thin lines will break) but firm enough to hold the shape.

To fill the piping bag, put in the nozzle, and then place the bag in a jug with the edges folded over the top. Spoon in icing to half-fill the bag and then fold over the edges carefully and press down the icing lightly so that it reaches the nozzle. Twist the top of the bag two or three times and hold the bag tightly over the twist so that pressure can be applied with the thumb. Steady the bag near the nozzle with the other hand, but only with the tips of the fingers. (If the second hand holds the bag tightly, this warms the icing and makes it sticky and unmanageable.)

Butter Icing

This quickly made icing can be spread or piped, and is generally used for sponge sandwiches and for assembling gâteaux.

Makes 350 g (12 oz) icing – to fill and cover one sponge sandwich
Time Preparation 5 minutes

Ingredients
125 g (4 oz) unsalted butter   flavouring
250 g (8 oz) icing sugar
2 tablespoons hot water,
    fruit juice or milk

Method
Put the butter into a bowl and cream it until soft. Sieve the icing sugar and gradually beat it into the butter, beating hard until well blended. Add the liquid and chosen flavouring and beat until very light and fluffy. The icing may be prepared very easily with an electric mixer or a food processor.

Variations
Lemon or Orange Icing: Add 1 teaspoon grated lemon or orange rind, and use fruit juice as the liquid in the above recipe.
Coffee Icing: Substitute 1 tablespoon coffee essence for half the water or milk.
Chocolate Icing: Add 1 tablespoon cocoa powder mixed with the hot water; or omit liquid and add 40 g (1½ oz) melted plain chocolate.

One-stage Soft Icing

Soft margarine may be used to make a creamy icing very quickly, but the proportions are slightly different from Butter Icing.

Makes 350 g (12 oz) icing – to fill and cover one sponge sandwich
Time Preparation 3 minutes

Ingredients
250 g (8 oz) icing sugar   flavouring (see variations
75 g (3 oz) soft margarine   below)
1 tablespoon milk or fruit
    juice

Method
Put all the ingredients into a mixing bowl and beat hard until the icing is soft and creamy.

Variations
Vanilla Icing: Add a few drops of vanilla essence to the icing.
Lemon or Orange Icing: Add 1 teaspoon grated lemon or orange rind, and use fruit juice as the liquid in the above recipe.
Coffee Icing: Substitute 1 tablespoon coffee essence for the milk or fruit juice.
Chocolate Icing: Add 1 tablespoon cocoa powder to the milk or fruit juice; or omit liquid and add 40 g (1½ oz) melted plain chocolate.

Glacé Icing

This quick, popular icing for sponge sandwiches, small cakes and biscuits may be used for writing on cakes but is not suitable for more elaborate piping.

Makes 125 g (4 oz) icing – to cover one sponge sandwich
Time Preparation 3 minutes

Ingredients
125 g (4 oz) icing sugar   flavouring and colouring
1–2 tablespoons warm
    water

Method
Sieve the sugar into a bowl. Add the water with flavouring and colouring, and stir well until completely mixed. The icing should coat the back of a spoon quite thickly, without being runny. Spread on the cake at once before the icing develops a crisp crust.

For *glossy icing,* put the ingredients into a small, heavy-based pan and heat until just warm, stirring to dissolve the sugar. This will give a smooth, shiny icing which looks very professional.

Variations
Coffee Icing: Add 1 teaspoon coffee essence.
Chocolate Icing: Dissolve 2 teaspoons cocoa powder in the water before adding to the sugar, and flavour with a few drops of vanilla essence.
Mocha Icing: Prepare Chocolate Icing, using coffee essence instead of vanilla.
Lemon or Orange Icing: Use fruit juice instead of water in the main recipe, and add a little of the appropriate colouring if liked.

Fondant Icing

This beautifully smooth, creamy icing should be used over Almond Paste. It is particularly suitable for gâteaux and small fancy cakes.

Makes 500 g (1 lb) icing
Time Preparation 30 minutes

Ingredients
500 g (1 lb) granulated sugar   ¼ teaspoon cream of tartar
150 ml (¼ pint) water

Method
Put the sugar and water into a large, heavy saucepan and heat gently without stirring until the sugar has dissolved. Bring to the boil and add the cream of tartar. Boil to 115°C/240°F (when a little of the mixture dropped into a cup of cold water can be formed into a soft ball with the fingers).

Pour the mixture into a bowl and leave it until it is cool and a skin has formed on top. Beat hard until the icing is thick, and turn on to a cold surface. Work with a round-bladed knife until the icing is thick and smooth and then knead with the hands to a thick, creamy consistency. If not needed immediately, put into a bowl and cover with Clingfilm.

To use the icing, put into a bowl over a pan of hot water and heat gently until the mixture is like thick cream. Pour over a cake covered or topped with almond paste, or use for dipping small cakes.

Simple Fondant Icing

This uncooked version of fondant icing is sometimes known as 'plastic icing' because it can easily be rolled out to fit a cake. When the icing has set firmly, butter icing may be piped on to decorate the cake.

Makes 500 g (1 lb) icing
Time Preparation 10 minutes

Ingredients
500 g (1 lb) icing sugar   3 tablespoons liquid glucose
1 egg white

Method
Sieve the icing sugar into a bowl, and add the egg white. Put the glucose into a cup standing in hot water, and leave until soft. Add the glucose to the bowl and work the ingredients to make a stiff paste. Turn the icing on to a board and knead well.

Roll out the icing on a board lightly dusted with cornflour, which will give it a shiny surface. To fit a cake, the icing should be rolled into a circle the size of the top of the cake plus enough to reach half-way down the sides.

Lift on to the cake and mould down the sides with the hands. Leave until firm before decorating. The icing may be flavoured with essences or with 40 g (1½ oz) cocoa powder substituted for 40 g (1½ oz) icing sugar.

Cream Cheese Icing

This light, fluffy icing is particularly good with carrot cakes or light fruit cakes, but it may also be used for tray bakes or sponge sandwiches.

Makes 300 g (10 oz) icing
Time Preparation 5 minutes

Ingredients
250 g (8 oz) icing sugar   1 egg white
75 g (3 oz) cream cheese   ½ teaspoon vanilla essence

Method
Sieve the icing sugar. Cream the cheese until light and smooth. Whisk the egg white until it forms soft peaks. Gradually cream the icing sugar into the cheese. Fold in the egg white. Flavour with vanilla essence, and spread on the cake immediately.

Variations
Lemon or Orange Icing: Omit the vanilla essence and flavour with 1 teaspoon grated fruit rind and a few drops of the appropriate essence, and colouring if liked.

American Frosting

This unusual and delicious icing, which looks like snow, has a slightly crisp surface but a soft interior. It is easiest to prepare with a hand-held electric whisk or an electric mixer.

Makes 250 g (8 oz) icing – to cover a 17.5 cm (7 in) cake
Time Preparation 30 minutes

Ingredients
250 g (8 oz) granulated sugar   1 egg white
4 tablespoons water

Method
Put the sugar and water into a thick pan, and heat gently until the sugar has dissolved. Boil to 115°C/240°F (when a little of the mixture dropped into a cup of cold water can be formed into a soft ball with the fingers).

In a large bowl, whisk the egg white until it forms stiff peaks. Remove the syrup from the heat and wait until the bubbles die down. Pour into the bowl in a slow, steady stream while continuing to whisk. The mixture will gradually thicken and become white and opaque when it is nearly cold. Pour quickly on to the cake and immediately swirl with a palette knife to form peaks. The icing sets very quickly, and must be placed on the cake just when it has the consistency of thick whipped cream.

Pour the syrup in a steady stream into the egg whites, whisking all the time.

Royal Icing

This is the traditional icing for wedding cakes and other special occasion cakes. The icing should be very white and hard enough to support decorations, and it should be applied over Almond Paste to prevent oils from the cake discolouring it. Leftover icing may be kept in a bowl covered with a damp cloth for up to 3 days to use as a second coat or for piping.

Makes 500 g (1 lb) icing
Time Preparation 20 minutes

Ingredients
2 egg whites
500 g (1 lb) icing sugar
1 tablespoon lemon juice

Method
Whisk the egg whites lightly to mix them, but do not beat to a light froth. Sieve the icing sugar and, using a very clean wooden spoon, gradually beat it into the egg whites. Add the lemon juice, and continue beating until the icing is very white and stands in peaks.

For coating a cake, the icing should be like softly whipped cream; for piping, it must stand in stiff, upright peaks. These effects are best achieved by hand-beating, as an electric mixer causes the formation of air bubbles which cannot be removed. For an icing which remains slightly soft, add 1 teaspoon glycerine.

To ice a cake, first prepare the Almond Paste (page 124), cover the cake with it and leave to dry. Put all the Royal Icing on top of the cake and gradually work it down over the cake, working from the centre with a palette knife. Spread the icing over the sides of the cake evenly, and then neaten the top surface with long sweeping movements of a straight-edged knife or ruler. Smooth the sides of the cake with vertical movements of the knife or ruler. For a smooth, crisp finish, it is best to use two thinner coats of icing, rather than one thick layer. The first coat must be completely dry before the second one is applied. Decorations should not be piped on until the top layer is completely dry.

Quantities for Cakes
○ One quantity of Royal Icing from the above recipe is enough for the top and sides of a 17.5 cm (7 in) cake, with a little left for piping.
○ Double quantities will be needed for two coats of icing for a 17.5 cm (7 in) cake, or for a single coat for a 22.5–25 cm (9–10 in) cake.

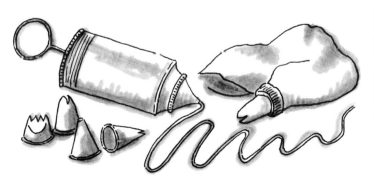

Using Confectioners' Custard to fill éclairs and tarts

Confectioners' Custard

Also known as pastry cream, this is a rich, thick custard used to fill choux pastry (e.g. éclairs), gâteaux and fruit tarts. It may also be mixed with an equal quantity of whipped cream to make a very rich filling.

Makes 450 ml (¾ pint) custard
Time Preparation 10 minutes

Ingredients
50 g (2 oz) caster sugar
2 egg yolks
2 tablespoons plain flour
2 tablespoons cornflour
300 ml (½ pint) milk
1 egg white
vanilla or coffee essence, to taste

Method
Put the sugar and egg yolks into a bowl and beat them until they are thick and pale. Beat in the flour and cornflour, and enough milk to make a smooth paste. Heat the remaining milk to boiling point, and pour it on to the egg mixture, stirring all the time. Return the mixture to the saucepan and stir over a low heat until the mixture just boils. Take off the heat.

Whisk the egg white until it forms stiff peaks and fold it into the custard. Return the saucepan to the heat and flavour the custard to taste with vanilla or coffee essence. Stir over low heat for 2 minutes. Leave until cold before using.

Chocolate Glaze

This easy icing with its rich flavour is ideal for chocolate cakes and sponge sandwiches, or for small cakes in paper cases.

Makes 175 g (6 oz) icing – to cover a 17.5 cm (7 in) cake
Time Preparation 10 minutes

Ingredients
65 g (2½ oz) plain chocolate, broken into pieces
65 g (2½ oz) icing sugar
2 tablespoons caster sugar
6 tablespoons boiling water

Method
Place the chocolate in a bowl over hot water. When the chocolate has melted, stir in the icing sugar and remove from the heat. Put the caster sugar and water into a small pan, stir well and then simmer for 5 minutes without stirring.

Pour the sugar syrup on to the chocolate and beat hard until the icing is of coating consistency. Pour on to the cake immediately.

Almond Paste

Also known as marzipan, this almond icing is used under Royal and Fondant Icing to protect the colour of these icings from the oils in rich cakes which can cause discoloration. Almond Paste should be placed over a thin glaze of jam on the cake, which protects the delicate colour of the almond mixture.

Makes 500 g (1 lb) almond paste
Time Preparation 10 minutes

Ingredients
125 g (4 oz) icing sugar
125 g (4 oz) caster sugar
250 g (8 oz) ground almonds
1 teaspoon lemon juice
few drops of almond essence
1 egg, beaten*

* 1–2 egg yolks alone may be used for Almond Paste, and the whites kept for the Royal Icing which covers it. 1–2 egg whites alone may be used for a very delicate Almond Paste.

Method
Sieve the icing sugar and stir it into the caster sugar and almonds until evenly coloured. Add the lemon juice and essence, and then the egg, and work together to give a firm paste. Knead lightly on a board sprinkled with icing sugar before rolling out to fit the cake, but do not overwork or the Almond Paste will become oily.

When the cake has been covered, the Almond Paste should be left to dry for 48 hours before Royal Icing is placed on top. If this is inconvenient, brush the Almond Paste with egg white and leave to dry for 15 minutes before covering with Royal Icing. The Almond Paste will remain soft, but this way it will not spoil the white icing.

Quantities for Cakes
○ One quantity of Almond Paste from the above recipe will coat the top only of a 20 cm (8 in) round or 17.5 cm (7 in) square cake. Double the quantity to coat the sides of the cake as well.

○ For the top of a 22.5 cm (9 in) round or 20 cm (8 in) square cake, increase the quantity of almonds to 300 g (10 oz) and other ingredients in proportion. Double these quantities to coat the sides of the cake as well.
○ For the top of a 25 cm (10 in) round or 22.5 cm (9 in) square cake, increase the quantity of almonds to 350 g (12 oz) and other ingredients in proportion. Double these quantities to coat the sides of the cake as well.

Praline

Praline is a delicious mixture of cooked sugar and toasted almonds which has to be finely crushed, and is then used as a topping for whipped cream and icings, or which may be used to flavour ice creams and other puddings.

Makes 125 g (4 oz) praline
Time Preparation 10 minutes

Ingredients
50 g (2 oz) caster sugar
50 g (2 oz) blanched almonds, chopped coarsely

Method
Put the sugar into a small, heavy pan. Heat gently without stirring for about 4 minutes until the sugar forms a deep-amber-coloured syrup. Spread the almonds on a baking sheet and toast them under a medium grill until golden-brown.

Stir the almonds into the sugar syrup and pour on to an oiled baking sheet or cold marble. Leave until completely cold. Break into large pieces and then crush into very small pieces with a rolling pin or in a blender. Use at once, or store in an airtight tin.

Chocolate Decorations

Chocolate decorations are easy to make, and give a professional finish to cakes. Cake-covering chocolate, chocolate dots and plain block chocolate are all suitable to use. Plain chocolate is easier to handle and sets more firmly than milk chocolate, and its dark colour looks more attractive as a contrast to icings. No liquid should be allowed to touch the chocolate during melting, or it will change the texture of it. The first stage of preparing chocolate decorations is melting the chocolate in a bowl over hot water, or in a microwave oven.

Chocolate curls (also known as Caraque) make a perfect topping for a cake covered with butter icing or chocolate glaze. Spread a thin layer of melted chocolate on a cold, firm surface such as marble or the heatproof top of a kitchen unit. Leave until just firm but not hard. Take a straight-bladed sharp knife and hold the point and handle. Place across the chocolate at an angle of 45° and gently draw away from the body, shaving off a curl of chocolate. Do not press into the chocolate or the pieces will be too thick and will not curl. Carefully lift the chocolate curls on to a plate and chill. Store in an airtight container.

Chocolate squares and triangles may be arranged in patterns standing upright or at an angle on cakes, or may be used to form a square 'box' around pieces of cake to make attractive petits fours. Chocolate cake-covering is easiest to use for this purpose. Draw a 15 cm (6 in) square on kitchen foil or baking parchment and place it on a flat surface. Melt 50 g (2 oz) chocolate and spread it thinly on the marked square. Leave until just set, and then use a ruler and sharp knife to cut it into 2.5 cm (1 in) or 5 cm (2 in) squares. Cut across to make triangles. Place on a flat baking sheet and chill until hard. Store in a container in a cold place for up to 2 weeks. *Fancy shapes* may be made in the same way, using sharp-edged petits fours or small biscuit cutters. When preparing squares, triangles or other shapes, always lift them with a knife, because fingers can mark the chocolate and remove the attractive shine.

Chocolate leaves look delightful, and are best made from cake-covering chocolate. Use well-shaped rose leaves or other attractive shapes, and wash and dry them thoroughly. Melt the chocolate and remove it from the heat. Use a fine paintbrush to coat the underside of the leaves with melted chocolate. Place chocolate-side upwards on a plate and chill until firm. Peel off the leaves carefully. Store in a container in a cold place for up to 2 weeks. Use the leaves individually as decoration, or arrange as a spray on a cake, piping a thin line of chocolate as a connecting stem.

Chocolate decorations and frosted flowers

Frosted Flowers

For long-term keeping, flowers may be crystallised with gum arabic and sugar, or with sugar syrup, but for short-term use it is much quicker to prepare them with a simple egg white and sugar method.

Choose fairly small flowers such as violets or primroses, or use rose petals and then reassemble them into complete flowers. Herb leaves, particularly mint, also look attractive. Avoid flowers which have grown from bulbs as these can be poisonous. The flowers must be clean and dry.

Put 1 egg white and 2 teaspoons cold water into a bowl and whisk until lightly frothy. Using a fine paintbrush, paint all over the flowers, back and front, until they are completely covered in egg white (do not dip the flowers into the egg white or they will become soggy and shapeless). Dust a sheet of greaseproof paper or baking parchment with caster sugar and place the flowers at intervals on the surface. Gently sprinkle with caster sugar to coat the flowers, and leave until dry. The flowers can be stored between layers of tissue paper for up to 4 weeks.

To make chocolate curls, angle the knife at 45° and draw it away from you across the chocolate.

Freezing Reminders

Nearly all baked goods freeze well, and it is worth baking extra quantities to freeze as this saves fuel and labour. When batch-baking, it is best not to overstrain machines or exhaust one's own energy. A double quantity of cake mixture or biscuits can be tackled easily by hand or machine; larger quantities are very difficult to mix. If four or six similar cakes are needed, it is quicker and easier to make a double quantity three times rather than to tackle a huge bowl of mixture.

It is not worth freezing fruit cakes or baked biscuits as these store very well in airtight tins or storage boxes. Fatless sponges should be eaten quickly and do not freeze well. It is always worth keeping bread and other yeast-bakes in the freezer for emergencies, while iced cakes may be prepared ahead for special occasions.

Bread
Freeze bread when it is freshly baked and cold, wrapped in freezer bags. White and brown breads store well for up to 4 weeks, but those with crisp crusts lose the crust which tends to break off after 1 week. Enriched breads such as milk breads, and fruit and malt loaves will keep in peak condition for up to 6 weeks.

Bread Doughs
Freeze batches of prepared dough in useful portions to fit standard tins (e.g. 500 g/1 lb), and pack in lightly oiled freezer bags, which must be tightly sealed to prevent a skin forming on the surface of the dough. Dough may be frozen before it has risen, and will keep for up to 8 weeks, but it will need 5–6 hours at room temperature before rising, kneading, shaping, proving again and baking. Risen dough may be frozen successfully for up to 3 weeks; kept frozen for longer than this, it will give poor results. This dough will need kneading, shaping, proving again and baking after 5–6 hours' thawing.

Part-baked Doughs
Part-baked rolls may be frozen successfully, but loaves are not good as during part-baking the crust becomes well-formed and coloured before the centre of the bread is set. To part-bake white or wholemeal rolls, place the shaped and risen rolls in a low oven (Gas Mark 2/150°C/300°F) for 20 minutes until set but pale. Cool and pack in usable quantities in freezer bags, packing carefully to prevent squashing the soft rolls. These will store for up to 4 months and they can then be baked while still frozen. Allow 20 minutes for baking white rolls (Gas Mark 6/200°C/400°F) or brown rolls (Gas Mark 8/230°C/450°F).

Other Yeast Bakes
Crumpets, croissants, brioches, teabreads, savarins and babas will all freeze well for up to 6 weeks. Pack savarins and babas in foil to prevent leakage of syrup; the smaller items can go into freezer bags. Danish pastries are best frozen un-iced if they are to be heated in the oven later, but iced pastries may be packed in a single layer to prevent smudging. Pizza may be frozen baked or unbaked.

Pastry
Unbaked pastry should be rolled and formed into a square, then wrapped in greaseproof paper and polythene before freezing. Baked pastry cases freeze well but must be carefully packed in boxes to prevent damage. Unbaked pastry will store well for up to 4 months, and baked pastry for up to 6 months.

Pies and Flans
Unbaked pies and flans may be frozen if a little care is taken. For fruit fillings, brush the surface of the bottom crust with egg white which will prevent sogginess. For meat fillings, brush the bottom crust with melted lard for the same reason. Air vents should not be cut in pastry before freezing, and the pies are best open-frozen before wrapping to prevent sogginess.

Fruit pies may be made with cooked or uncooked filling, but apples tend to brown if stored in a pie for more than 4 weeks. Meat pies are best made with a cooked filling and uncooked pastry. To bake the pies, cut slits in the top crust and bake unthawed as for fresh pies, allowing about 10 minutes longer than the normal cooking time.

Baked pies may be frozen and are best prepared in a foil container, or in a rustproof and crack-proof container. Wrap in foil or a freezer bag for freezing. A cooked pie should be reheated at Gas Mark 5/190°C/375°F for 40–50 minutes for a double-crust pie, or 30–50 minutes for a one-crust pie, depending on size. Cooked pies may also be eaten thawed but not reheated, as may sausage rolls and pasties.

Scones and Griddle-cakes
Pack in usable quantities, such as sixes or dozens, in freezer bags. Reheat in a moderate oven (Gas Mark 4/180°C/350°F) or microwave oven.

Small Cakes
Plain cakes such as Sponge Drops may be packed in bags in usable quantities, and they thaw quickly. Choux pastry éclairs and meringues may be frozen unfilled and are best packed in boxes to prevent crushing. Choux pastry may also be frozen ready-filled with sweetened whipped cream or ice cream; they can be iced quickly when thawed.

Sponge Sandwiches
While fatless sponges do not freeze well, those containing butter make useful standbys. Single layers may be frozen in pairs, with a piece of foil between for easy separation, then wrapped in foil or a freezer bag. These layers may be thawed and freshly filled with jam, cream or icing. Cakes frozen with a jam filling will become rather soggy in the centre. Butter-iced cakes should be open-frozen before wrapping, and if they are very delicate, they are best packed in a box. To prevent the icing cracking, a cake may be frozen on a cake board and lifted straight into the box for storage. It is better not to put on decorations such as sugar flowers or silver balls as these will discolour when thawed as moisture forms on them.

Biscuits
Crisply baked biscuits keep best in a tin or other airtight container and do not need freezing. Unbaked biscuit dough, however, freezes well, wrapped in foil or a freezer bag. If it is formed into a cylinder before freezing, slices may be cut off while the dough is still hard and can be baked at once into light, crisp biscuits.

*I*ndex

Page numbers in italics indicate illustrations; the abbreviation (m/w) indicates that a recipe is for microwave baking.

A

Almond paste, 124
Almonds, ground *See* Ground almonds
American frosting, 122
Apple crisps, 76
Apple pie, Norfolk, 83, *83*
Apple strudel, *64*, 74
Apple walnut cake (m/w), 31, *31*
Autumn fruit pie, 84, *84*

B

Bacon and egg flans, spiced, 69, *69*
Bagels, 45, *45*
Baking equipment
  basic essentials, 11–12
  electrical equipment, 12, 14
  microwave ovens, 29
  ovens, 12, 14
  papers, 12
  tins, 12, 17, 104, 109
Baking ingredients, basic, 8, 9, 15
Banana and cherry loaf, 102
Banana bars, 103, *103*
Banana teabread (m/w), *32*, 35
Bath buns, 49, 50
Biscuit cake (m/w), *27*, 36
Biscuit making, 12, 86, 126
Biscuits
  bosworth jumbles, 88, *90*
  cheese thins, 93, *93*
  chocolate butter rings, 87, *87*
  chocolate sandwich biscuits, 89, *90*
  Cornish fairings, 89, *90*
  Easter biscuits, 87
  flapjacks (m/w), 36
  gingerbread men, 88, *88*
  golf biscuits, 93, *93*
  honey flapjacks, 94
  lemon crisps, 87, *87*
  macaroons, 88, *88*
  nutty fingers (m/w), 35, *35*
  petticoat tails, 89, *90*
  refrigerator biscuits, 94
  sailor hats, *85*, 92
  semi-sweet (m/w), 35
  shortbread, 94
  Viennese biscuits, *85*, 92
  walnut chocolate circles, *85*, 92
Blue cheese quiche, 79, *80*
Bosworth jumbles, 88, *90*
Brandy snaps, 113, *113*

Bread making
  flour for, 8
  freezing dough, 126
  general procedures, 15–16
  history of, 38
  microwave, rising in, 29
Breads
  See also Teabreads
  bagels, 45, *45*
  brioches, 44, *45*
  buttery rowies, 43, *43*
  calzone, 47, *47*
  challah, 45, *46*
  chapati, 48, *48*
  cheese bread, 42
  cheese bread rolls, *37*, 42
  croissants, 44
  flowerpot bread, 39, *40*
  French flutes, 39, *40*
  grissini, 47, *47*
  milk twist, 42, *front cover*
  nan, 48, *48*
  oaten loaf, *40*, 42
  pitta pockets, 46
  poppy seed twists, 43, *43*
  pumpernickel, 46, *46*
  rye bread, *40*, 42
  spoon bread, 59, *59*
  Swedish limpa, 46
  white bread, 38
  wholemeal bread, *37*, 39
Brioches, 44, *45*
Buffet horns, 69, *70*
Buns
  Bath buns, *49*, 50
  Chelsea buns, *52*, 56
  raspberry buns, 109, *109*
Butter, use of, 9
Butter icing, 121
Buttermilk, 9
Butterscotch brownies, 110
Buttery rowies, 43, *43*

C

Cake-making
  decorations, 125
  freezing, advice on, 126
  general methods, 16–18
  historical note, 96
  icings, 120–124
  microwave, 28–29
  no-bake cakes, 24–26
  testing in baking, 17
  tins for, 17
Cakes
  See also Cakes, small; Gâteaux
  apple walnut cake (m/w), 31, *31*
  banana and cherry loaf, 102
  banana bars, 103, *103*
  biscuit cake (m/w), *27*, 36
  brandy snaps, 113, *113*
  carrot cake, 102
  carrot cake (m/w), 31, *32*
  chocolate almond cake, *95*, 108
  chocolate cake (m/w), 30, *31*
  chocolate marble cake, 107, *107*
  chocolate rum cake, 108, *front cover*
  Christmas log cake, 114, *116*
  Christmas tree gâteau, 114, *114*
  coconut cake, 100, *100*
  Colchester gingerbread, 97, *98*
  country wholemeal cake, *98*, 101
  crunch cake, 109, *109*
  cupcakes (m/w), 34, *34*
  dark chocolate cake, 106

Dundee cake, 100, *100*
éclairs, *116*, 118
farmhouse fruit cake (m/w), 30
fruit gâteau, 115, *116*
gâteau St Honoré, *111*, 115
Genoese sponge, 106
geranium sponge, 105, *105*
honey loaf, 102
lemon sponge (m/w), 30, *32*
marmalade cake (m/w), *27*, 30
meringues, 112, *113*
milk chocolate cake, 107, *107*
mocha cake, 108
nutty loaf, 101
orange walnut cake, 97, *98*
praline cream gâteau, 115, *116*
rich fruit cake, 118, *119*
seed cake, 97, *98*
sherry almond cake, 97
sponge cakes, 104–106
Swiss roll, 105, *105*
Victoria sponge sandwich, 104
whisked sponge, 105
wholefood cakes, 101–103
wholemeal sponge sandwich, 103, *103*
Cakes, small
  butterscotch brownies, 110
  chocolate delights (m/w), *32*, 36
  crunch cake, 109, *109*
  cup cakes (m/w), 34, *34*
  lemon crust squares, *95*, 110
  melting moments, 110
  queen cakes, 110
  raspberry buns, 109, *109*
  sponge drops, *95*, 104
Calories, 11
Calzone, *47*, 47
Caraque, 125
Carbohydrates, 10
Carrot cake
  basic, 102
  microwave, 31, *32*
Cereals, 8
Challah, 45, *46*
Chapati, 48, *48*
Cheese
  blue cheese quiche, 79, *80*
  cheese and nut bread, 51, *51*
  cheese bread, 42
  cheese pastry, 68
  cheese bread rolls, *37*, 42
  cheese thins, 93, *93*
Chelsea buns, *52*, 56
Cherry loaf, banana and, 102
Chocolate biscuits
  chocolate butter rings, 87, *87*
  chocolate sandwich biscuits, 89, *90*
  walnut chocolate circles, *85*, 92
Chocolate cake (m/w), 30, *31*
Chocolate cakes
  almond cake, *95*, 108
  chocolate cake (m/w), 30, *31*
  chocolate delights, (m/w), *32*, 36
  cup cakes, (m/w), 34
  dark chocolate cake, 106
  éclairs, *116*, 118
  fudge flan, 26
  marble cake, 107, *107*
  microwave, 30, *31*
  milk chocolate cake, 107, *107*
  mocha cake, 108
  no-bake, 26
  rum cake, 108, *front cover*
  tiffin, 25, *25*
  truffle cakes, 26
Chocolate decorations, 125, *125*

Chocolate glaze, 124
Chocolate icing, 121
Christmas cake, no-bake, 25, *25*
Christmas log cake, 114, *116*
Christmas tree gâteau, 114, *114*
Choux pastry, 118
Cider loaf, 55
Classic quiche lorraine, 77, 82
Clifton puffs, 75, 76
Coconut cake, 100, *100*
Coffee cup cakes, (m/w), 34
Coffee éclairs, *116*, 118
Coffee flavouring, 9
Coffee icing, 121
Colchester gingerbread, 97, *98*
Confectioners' custard, 123, *123*
Cornish fairings, 89, *90*
Cornish pasties, 70, 72
Country wholemeal cake, 98, 101
Crab puffs, 70, 72
Cream cheese icing, 122
Croissants, 44
Crumpets, *57*, 58
Crunch cake, 109, *109*
Cumberland currant slice, 73, *73*
Cup cakes (m/w), 34, *34*

D

Danish pastries, *60*, 64
Dark chocolate cake, 106
Date and nut loaf (m/w), 34, *34*
Decorations for cakes, 125
Derbyshire pikelets, 59, *60*
Doughnuts, Greek, *60*, 63
Dried fruit, 9
Drop scones, *19*, 20
Dundee cake, 100, *100*

E

Easter biscuits, 87
Eclairs, *116*, 118
Eggs, use of, 9
Eggs in sponge cakes, 104
Electrical equipment, 12, 14
Essences, 9

F

Farmhouse fruit cake (m/w), 30
Fats, 9, 10
Fisherman's puff, *80*, 82
Flaky pastry, 67
Flan making, 78, 126
Flans
  See also Pies; Tarts and tartlets
  spiced bacon and egg, 69
  tomato and onion, 79
Flapjacks, honey, 94
Flapjacks (m/w), 36
Flavourings, 9
Flour, 8, 15
Flowerpot bread, 39, *40*
Fondant icing, 122
Food processors, 12, 14, 104
French flutes, 39, *40*
Freezing procedures, 126
Frosted flowers, 125
Frostings *See* Icings
Fruit, dried, 9
Fruit biscuit cake, *21*, 24
Fruit cake (m/w), 30
Fruit cake, rich, 118, *119*
Fruit cup cakes (m/w), 34
Fruit gâteau, 115, *116*

Fruit pies and tarts
  apple crisps, 76
  Autumn fruit pie, 84, *84*
  glazing methods, 79
  Norfolk apple pie, 83, *83*
  orange cream tart, 84, *84*
  summer fruit tarts, *65*, 73

G

Game pie, 77, 83
Gâteaux
  Christmas tree gâteau, 114,
    114
  fruit gâteau, 115, *116*
  gâteau St Honoré, *111*, 115
  praline cream gâteau, 115, *116*
Genoese sponge, 106
Geranium sponge, 105, *105*
Gingerbread, Colchester, 97, *98*
Gingerbread men, 88, *88*
Glacé icing, 121
Golf biscuits, 93, *93*
Greek doughnuts in honey syrup,
  60, 63
Griddle cakes, freezing, 126
Griddle scones, 21, *22*
Griddles, 20
Grissini, 47, *47*

H

Honey flapjacks, 94
Honey loaf, 102

I

Icing cakes, 120–124
Icings
  almond paste, 124
  American frosting, 122
  chocolate glaze, 124
  cream cheese icing, 122
  flavourings, 121–122
  fondant icing, 122
  glacé icing, 121
  one-stage soft icing, 121
  royal icing, 123
  simple fondant icing, 122
Ingredients, basic, 8, 9, 15
Italian torrone, *19*, 26

K

Kugelhopf, *60*, 62

L

Lardy cake, 51, *51*
Lemon crisps, 87, *87*
Lemon crust squares, *95*, 110
Lemon cup cakes (m/w), 34
Lemon icing, 121, 122
Lemon sponge (m/w), 30, *32*
Liquids in baking, 9, 15

M

Macaroons, 88, *88*
Maids of honour, 73, *73*
Margarine, 9
Marmalade cake, (m/w), 27, 30

Marzipan, 124
May Day tarts, 75, *75*
Measuring equipment, 11
Measuring quantities, note on, 4
Melting moments, 110
Meringues, 112, *113*
Microwave baking, 28–36
Milk chocolate cake, 107, *107*
Milk twist, 42, *front cover*
Minerals, in nutrition, 10–11
Mixers, food, 12
Mocha cake, 108
Mocha icing, 121

N

Nan, 48, *48*
No-bake chocolate cake, 26
No-bake Christmas cake, 25, *25*
Norfolk apple pie, 83, *83*
Nutrition, 10–11
Nutty fingers (m/w), 35, *35*
Nutty loaf, 101

O

Oatcakes, 21, *22*
Oaten loaf, *40*, 42
One-stage soft icing, 121
Orange cream tart, 84, *84*
Orange cup cakes (m/w), 34
Orange icing, 121, 122
Orange walnut cake, 97, *98*
Ovens, 12, 14

P

Panettone, *52*, 54
Papers for baking, 12
Pastry
  cheese, 68
  choux, 118
  flaky, 67
  puff, 68
  rough puff, 68
  shortcrust, 66
  sweet shortcrust, 67
  wholemeal shortcrust, 67
Pastry cream, 123
Pastry making, 12, 18, 66–68,
  126
Pateley fritters, 59, *59*
Petticoat tails, 89, *90*
Pie making, 78–79, 127
Pies
See also Tarts and tartlets
  Autumn fruit pie, 84, *84*
  game pie, 77, 83
  Norfolk apple pie, 83, *83*
  steak, kidney and mushroom
    pie, *80*, 82
Pikelets, Derbyshire, 59, *60*
Piping, 121
Pitta pockets, 46
Poppy seed twists, 43, *43*
Potato scones, 21
Praline, 124
Praline cream gâteau, 115, *116*
Proteins, 10
Puff pastry, 68
Pumpernickel, 46, *46*

Q

Queen cakes, 110
Quiche, blue cheese, 79, *80*
Quiche lorraine, 77, 82

R

Raising agents, 8
Raspberry buns, 109, *109*
Refrigerator biscuits, 94
Rich fruit cake, 118, *119*
Rough puff pastry, 68
Royal icing, 123
Rum babas, *57*, 63
Rye bread, *40*, 42

S

Saffron bread, *52*, 54
Sailor hats, *85*, 92
Sausage rolls, special, *70*, 72
Savarin, 62, *62*
Scones
  drop scones, *19*, 20
  griddle scones, 21, *22*
  potato scones, 21
  Scots treacle scones, 55, *55*
Seed cake, 97, 98
Selkirk bannock, *49*, 51
Semi-sweet biscuits (m/w), 35, *35*
Sherry almond cake, 97
Shortbread, 89, 94
Shortcrust pastry, 66
Simple fondant icing, 122
Singin' hinny, *22*, 24
Small cakes, *See* Cakes, small
Smoked haddock vol-au-vents,
  69, *69*
Spiced bacon and egg flans, 69, *69*
Spiced raisin flan, *21*, 25
Spices, use of, 9
Sponge cake, whisked, 105
Sponge cake making, 104, 126
Sponge drops, *95*, 104
Sponge sandwich, Victoria, 104
Sponge sandwich, wholemeal,
  103, *103*
Spoon bread, 59, *59*
Steak, kidney and mushroom pie,
  80, 82
Strawberry hearts, *65*, 74
Sugar, 9, 104
Summer fruit tarts, *65*, 73
Swedish limpa, 46
Sweet shortcrust pastry, 67
Swiss roll, 105, *105*

T

Tarts and tartlets
  apple crisps, 76
  glazing methods, 79
  maids of honour, 73, *73*
  May Day tarts, 75, *75*
  orange cream tart, 84, *84*
  summer fruit tarts, *65*, 73
Teabreads
  banana and cherry loaf, 102
  banana teabread (m/w), *32*, 35
  cheese and nut bread, 51, *51*
  cider loaf, 55
  date and nut loaf (m/w), 34, *34*
  honey loaf, 102
  lardy cake, 51, *51*
  panettone, *52*, 54
  saffron bread, *52*, 54
  Selkirk bannock, *49*, 51
Teisen lap, *22*, 24
Tiffin, 25, *25*
Tins, 12, 17, 104, 109
Tomato and onion flan, 79, *80*
Treacle scones, Scots, 55, *55*

V

Vanilla icing, 121
Vanilla pod, use of, 9
Victoria sponge sandwich, 104
Viennese biscuits, *85*, 92
Vitamins, 10–11
Vol-au-vents, 69, 82

W

Walnut cake, orange, 97, *98*
Walnut chocolate circles, *85*, 92
West country cream splits, *52*, 56
White bread, 38
Whisked sponge, 105
Wholefood cakes, 101–103
Wholemeal bread, 37, 39
Wholemeal cake, country, *98*,
  101
Wholemeal shortcrust pastry, 67
Wholemeal sponge sandwich,
  103, *103*

Y

Yeast
  pastry and batter bakes, 58–64
  procedures for using, 15
  types of, 8–9
Yeast dough
  freezing, 126
  microwave, proving in, 29
  procedure for making, 15–16
Yorkshire fat rascals, 55, *55*